NEW
AFRICAN
FASHION

HELEN JENNINGS

NEW
AFRICAN
FASHION

PRESTEL
Munich • London • New York

CONTENTS

by Iké Udé

FOREWORD

In 1907 the storied, iconic oracle of modern art, Pablo Diego José Francisco de Paula Juan Nepomuceno María de los Remedios Cipriano de la Santísima Trinidad Ruiz y Picasso, simply known as Picasso, had an 'African moment'.

It was his very first encounter with African art. The sublimely grotesque masks, nail-studded fetishes, scar-cheeked idols and distorted/disfigured human representations he saw were like nothing he'd ever witnessed or learned about in Europe or the East. This shocking encounter arrested his imagination. Soon after, he began and finished work on *Les Demoiselles d'Avignon*. This masterpiece marked a paradigm shift, a *tabula rasa* for a radically new kind of modernism with an African foundation!

In fashion, a bevy of designers from Yves Saint Laurent, Junya Watanabe, Ralph Lauren, Marc Jacobs and John Galliano to Alexander McQueen, Comme des Garçons and Jean Paul Gaultier have all quoted African art in part or *in toto*. Evidently, African art or African fashion is not new – quite the contrary. What is relatively new on the global stage are African artists and fashion designers deservedly operating with a creative autonomy that has not been seen before.

Enter the new or not-so-new African designers:

Xuly Bët by Lamine Badian Kouyaté came to public attention in the early 1990s and shook the fashion world with his seemingly Dada/punk attitude that, as it turned out, was culturally astute, economically informed and a seminal fashion moment. Xuly Bët's genius wasn't just that he recycled second-hands but that, like an excellent artist, he transformed what he found – one of the core lessons that Picasso learned from African art – to transform rather than transcribe.

The princely *arbiter elegantiarum* Ozwald Boateng is well noted to have alighted on Savile Row and peeled several layers of stodginess off the traditional home of bespoke tailoring. With an aesthete's eye for suppleness of syntax, he infused his fitted suits, by turns, with whispery hues or shades of purple, green, red and at times with iridescent effects, while fastidiously indulging his Ashanti/Ghanaian disposition for bold, marvellous colours in the lining of the jackets.

Amaka Osakwe of Maki Oh is quite the darling and inventive maverick. There is in her work a clear gift of craftsmanship, sympathy for African sartorial classics, the impishness of the coquette, the insouciance of Fela's 'Shakara' and a wonderfully infectious 'girls-just-wanna-have-fun attitude'. Thanks to Maki Oh, African girls, and increasingly their counterparts abroad, are having such fun wearing her clothes.

Lawyer turned designer Duro Olowu's prodigious, promiscuous appetite for and command of patterns and colours fondly echoes Henri Matisse, a Picasso contemporary who had his 'African moment', too.

The idiosyncratic, charming Adrien Sauvage is perhaps one of the wittiest designers working now, and surely a beacon of hope for loads of men who are sartorially challenged.

To be sure, the general Cubistic approach and detail-obsessed construction evident in the work of South Africa's Black Coffee label, designed by Jacques van der Watt, winningly quotes Picasso's African period with piquant poeticisms.

It was in 1907, Picasso admitted to the venerable French writer André Malraux, that he was so utterly stunned by his encounter with African art that he kept repeating the words 'shock', 'revelation', 'force' and 'charge'. Collectively, the varied superb talents of designers ranging from the veterans Joe Casely-Hayford and Eric Raisina to new talents Gloria Wavamunno, Mataano, Pierre-Antoine Vettorello and Stiaan Louw are all by various degrees inevitably holding sway on a global scale – for good. Consequently, as happened to Picasso aeons ago, the fashion world is increasingly having its 'African moment' in this new millennium.

Helen Jennings's book, *New African Fashion* – a first of its kind – frames this momentous, flowering movement beautifully and prefigures that inevitability, the 'African moment'. Hers is an immeasurably overdue, much-needed book and utterly to the point! To all these protean, magnificently inspired designers, I say *chapeau* and keep at it!

Iké Udé was born in Nigeria and moved to the US in the 1980s. He lives and works in New York City. His artwork is in the permanent collections of the Solomon Guggenheim Museum, New York, the Smithsonian National Museum, Washington DC, and numerous private collections. Udé is the founder and publisher of aRUDE magazine, a quarterly devoted to art, culture, style and fashion. He is the author of Style File: The World's Most Elegantly Dressed, *a comprehensive monograph recently released by HarperCollins. A style icon, he was selected as one of* Vanity Fair's 2009 International Best Dressed Originals.

Africa is fashion's new frontier. Having been sidelined by mainstream fashion for over half a century as little more than a source of aesthetic inspiration, the continent's home-grown industry is now showing the world how African fashion is really done. Today's generation of talented designers and image-makers are riding the broader wave of interest in Africa's renaissance and attracting an international clientele by balancing contemporary fashion's pursuit of the new with an appreciation of the ideals of beauty and adornment that are deeply rooted in Africa's cultural and social consciousness. This new guard, which includes labels and designers such as Lagos's Jewel by Lisa, Johannesburg's Black Coffee, Accra's Christie Brown, London's Duro Olowu and New York's Mataano, is creating the most exciting and original chapter in fashion's discourse since Japan emerged as a major player in the 1980s, and helping to give African style its moment in the sun.

The history of fashion in Africa is one of constant exchange and appropriation, a complex though ill-documented journey with different influences coming into play across time and place. Contrary to the accepted view of African traditions as monolithic and unchanging, the evolution of dress practices and sartorial acumen confirms fashion's role as a potent visual expression of a continent in constant flux. African aesthetics have travailed through empires, conflicts, slavery, migration, globalisation and urbanisation to cater to new contexts and markets. Body adornment – including clothing and accessories, tattoos, scarification, body painting and coiffures – has therefore fulfilled manifold roles. Serving as basic protection as well as a signifier of status, ambitions, beliefs and ethnic group, it becomes a second skin that gives the individual safe passage through the pageantry and also ceremonies that mark each stage of life. It also exposes a dedication to looking à la mode regardless of one's means or circumstances.

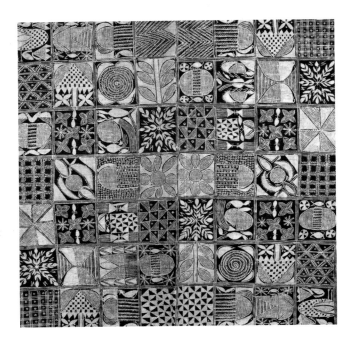

Woman's starch-resist adire eleko wrapper cloth, c. 1960, Yoruba, Nigeria

The earliest wearable African artefacts originate from Egypt, Nigeria, Cameroon and Sierra Leone, with some evidence dating back to 2000 BC and beyond. The practice of draping a single uncut length of cloth around the body formed the foundation of African dress. Arabian and Berber trade routes helped spread loom-spun textile technologies across Africa and from the 16th century onward, European travellers documented the changing tastes in fabrics, jewellery and other finery. In his 1874 book *The Heart of Africa*, Russian botanist Dr Georg Schweinfurth wrote of the east African Dinka tribe: 'Heavy rings load their wrists and ankles, clank and resound like the fetters of slaves. Free from any domination … They are not free from the fetters of fashion.' The Venetian glass bead trade in southern Africa was also certainly subject to the vagaries of fashion, with salesmen having to keep up with local tastes.

Cloth has acted as currency, gift, dowry, symbol of power, artisanal identity, method of communication and spiritual protection. Raffia, bark, woven, wax-printed and tie and dye varieties abound. Nigerian adire, for example, is a resist-dyed indigo cloth developed by Yoruba women in the 1800s. There are over 400 recognisable patterns, which are either hand-painted or stencilled onto the cloth before it is repeatedly immersed in the seductively deep-blue dye. Each symbol has an accepted meaning, giving a voice to the fabric and its wearer. Nigerian textile artist Nike Davies Okundaye teaches adire-making as a means of self-empowerment for women and emerging designer Maki Oh contemporises it for a modern audience.

Indigenous fabrics have survived and adapted to the introduction of cheaper industrially made products and imports of luxury fabrics including lace, silk, velvet and damask. In the late 19th century Dutch textile manufactures entered the market with a product that mimicked Asian batik fabrics.

INTRODUCTION

It was originally aimed at consumers in the Dutch East Indies (present-day Indonesia), but proved more popular in central and western Africa, and so companies quickly tailored their designs accordingly. Vlisco was and remains the market leader with its patented Wax Hollandais fabric. 'It's made in the Netherlands yet Africans feel like it's their product, which is magical', says Vlisco's Ester Huigen. 'Our design teams take inspirations from Africa and combine these with what's going on globally to create each collection.' Vlisco makes four womenswear and fabric collections a year and has also collaborated with designers including Lanre Da Silva Ajayi, Gilles Touré and Anggy Haif.

It currently competes with local and Asian printed fabrics, called fancy, Ankara or simply African print, which feature designs varying from the abstract to depicting political leaders and everyday objects. Originally the fabric of the poor, it has become the exemplar African fabric and having made it onto the runways of LAMB and Jean Paul Gaultier, it's seen as a high-fashion material by designers worldwide.

As foreigners settled in Africa, locals adopted and transformed the outsiders' styles of dress. Billowing and embroidered gowns, such as the boubou, agbada, riga and caftan, are considered the archetypal West African garments, yet are testament to the Islamic influence in the region since the 18th century. Bowler hats and walking sticks remain a staple for chiefs in the Niger Delta, having been introduced by British colonists in the 19th century. And the Ghanaian kaba combines an African-style wrapped skirt with a European-style blouse. The top half was originally encouraged by Christian missionaries who wished women to cover up their bare breasts. The ensemble remains popular and is viewed as entirely African.

Missionaries also helped to teach tailoring skills and in studios across Africa tailors now form the frontline of fashion, with those in Dakar and Bamako especially renowned. Before fashion design was a recognised profession, seamstresses and tailors were the ones who fed trends – and today's designers, most of whom operate from workshop-based production, remain reliant on their skills.

FASHION IN FOCUS

The back catalogue of Africa's celebrated 20th-century photographers tells us more than any history book about African style. Malian photographer Seydou Keïta (1921–2001) attracted the whole of Bamako society to his studio between 1948 and 1962. His formal yet intimate portraits employed an array of backdrops and props (everything

Clockwise from top left: The Peau de Léopard collection by Vlisco; The Nouvelle Histoire collection by Vlisco; Woman's bogolanfini, mud cloth, skirt, c.1990, Bamana people, Beledougou region, Mali; Woman's aso oke wrapper cloth, 19th century, Yoruba, Nigeria. The magenta thread is silk from the trans-Saharan caravan trade; Man's adinkra wrapper cloth, for funeral attire, c. 1960, Asante, Ghana; The Nouvelle Histoire collection by Vlisco; The Sparkling Grace collection by Vlisco

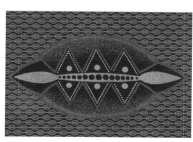
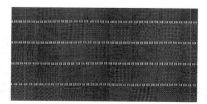

from a flower to a Vespa) to add an aspirational air to his subjects, who wore either African robes and headwraps or Western suits and army uniforms. Each image is a black and white memoir of a city's reinvention of itself in the face of unrelenting modernity.

His fellow citizen Malick Sidibé photographed Bamako's post-colonial youth in the 1960s and 1970s. Whether doing the Twist at a party, play-fighting on the beach or posing with their favourite James Brown records, his subjects wore the latest flares and minidresses with pride – and would flock to his studio the following week to marvel at the magical gelatin silver prints of themselves. Sidibé was commissioned by *The New York Times Magazine* to recreate his studio portraits for a fashion shoot in 2009. At first glance they look like images from his archive, but upon closer inspection the models (his family and friends) are wearing garments from Spring/Summer 2009 collections by the likes of Bottega Veneta, Chloé, Duro Olowu and Dries Van Noten.

Jean Depara (1928–1997) chronicled the elan of Kinshasa, Democratic Republic of Congo. In 1954 he was made the official photographer of rumba singer Franco, which allowed him to stalk the city's night spots, his camera strapped across him 'like a bow', in search of well-dressed, badly behaved revellers. Polka, tango and rumba resonated through the city, bringing a multi-ethnic crowd together.

Nigeria's J. D. Okhai Ojeikere chronicled 'moments of beauty' to create an artistic commentary on ethnographic change. He is best known for his Hairstyles series, which began in 1968 and includes around 1,000 headshots of fanciful braided up-dos and geles. Shot mainly from behind, these abstract images freeze the ephemeral and celebrate the admirable lengths to which African women go in the name of looking good.

Samuel Fosso grew up in Nigeria but fled to Bangui, Central African Republic, to escape the Biafran War. By day he shot paying customers at his studio yet by night he turned the camera on himself. Fosso's elaborate self-portraits began as narcissistic attempts at looking cool in his 1970s fashions (tight shirts, dark glasses, hot pants) but developed to incorporate

costumes, make-up and sets to transform himself into different characters. In *The Liberated American Woman of the 70s* he wears heels and a Stetson while in *The Chief who Sold Africa to the Colonialists* he's on his throne, sunflowers in his hand where his spear should be.

All these photographers were engrossed by an African youth culture that was in full bloom at the time when hipsters were hopeful for their

futures and engaged in a dialogue with international fashion and music trends. Today's leading African photographic artists, such as Andrew Dosunmu, Nontsikelelo 'Lolo' Veleko, Koto Bolofo, Iké Udé, Chris Saunders and Hassan Hajjaj, each have their own unique practices that will leave behind the cultural documents for fashion historians of the future.

Seydou Keïta, Untitled, *1959, gelatin silver print*

Left: Shade Fahm designs

Right: Styling by Oumou Sy, 1999

GENERATION THEN

Building upon past centuries of fashion development, the first generation of recognised fashion designers drew on local fabrics and styles as a means of showing pride in their African identities in the wake of a flurry of independence that swept across Africa in the 1960s. This in turn attracted international consumers, not least African-Americans who were engaged in the Civil Rights movement and who adopted African attire and hairstyles under the rallying cry of 'Black is Beautiful'.

Nigerian designer Shade Thomas-Fahm trained at Central Saint Martins in London, where she also worked as a model. She returned to Lagos in 1960 to launch the Shade's Boutique chain, offering modern versions of traditional garments. The pre-tied gele, turning iro and buba into a zip-up wrapper skirt and adapting a man's agbada into a woman's embroidered boubou were all her fashion firsts. 'At the time Nigerian women wore imported dresses, they thought African wear was their mothers' thing. But I was young and my dreams were tall', she says. Fahm was patronised by Nigerian royalty and professional women alike and sold worldwide. Abah Folawiyo, Betti O and Folorunsho Alakija join her in Nigeria's fashion's archive.

Pathé Ouédraogo grew up in Burkina Faso and opened his studio in Côte d'Ivoire in 1977. His label, Pathé'O, focused on modernised bubus and pagnes and has become presidential wear for leaders including Nelson Mandela. Malian Chris Seydou (1949–1994) achieved acclaim in Paris and across West Africa for his innovative use of bogolanfini. The mudcloth is made by Bamana women and is distinguished by its brown and white geometric patterns. It is believed to absorb *nyama*, a dangerous energy released while hunting and during circumcision ceremonies. Seydou was the first to turn it into a fashion fabric in the 1970s. While respecting its ritual significance, he carefully adjusted it to make Western styles. Today the Groupe Bogolan Kasobané, a collective of artists headed up by Kandioura Coulibaly, keep the fabric alive.

Ghanaian Tetteh Adzedu began the menswear label Adzedu of Shapes in Accra in the 1980s, where he also established a fashion school and was president of the Ghana Fashion Designers' Association. Fellow Ghanaian Kofi Ansah graduated from the Chelsea School of Art in 1977 and is now considered one of the forefathers of Ghanaian fashion. His Art Dress line incorporates kente, the famous woven fabric invented for the Ashante royalty, and adinkra, a printed cloth associated with Akan funerals, into his designs.

Niger designer Seidnally Sidhamed, better known as Alphadi, co-founded the Fédération Africaine des Créateurs and in 1998 launched the Festival International de la Mode Africaine (FIMA) in the Niger desert, a landmark African fashion exposition bringing African and international designers together. His award-winning designs reference nomadic tribes. Oumou Sy is a celebrated Senegalese costume and fashion designer who founded the Carnival of Dakar in the 1990s. Her fantastical creations are often excessively decorated, both with the beautiful (feathers, embroidery, amber beads) and the absurd (CDs, perfume bottles, calabashes), and turn their wearers into goddess-like symbols of African power and liberation. And in South Africa, Errol Arendz and Marianne Fassler entered the fashion scene in the 1980s and remain major players, having cemented their reputation as founders of contemporary fashion in the country.

Yves Saint Laurent,
1967

THE FRENCH CONNECTION

Yves Saint Laurent was undoubtedly the first internationally acclaimed fashion designer of African descent. He was born in Oran, Algeria, in 1936, a place he described as 'a town glittering in a patchwork of all colours under the sedate North African sun', and in later life he spent much of his time in Marrakech, where he owned the Jardin Majorelle. His designs repeatedly drew on the continent. His landmark Spring/Summer 1967 African collection featured a series of revealing shift dresses made from raffia, wooden beads and shells (a look re-imagined by Dolce & Gabbana in 2005 and by Gucci in 2011). *Harper's Bazaar* described it at the time as 'a fantasy of primitive genius – shells and jungle jewellery clustered to cover the bosom and hips, latticed to bare the midriff'. The following year he invented the safari jacket and successive collections included his take on tunics, caftans, djellabahs and turbans.

Yves Saint Laurent has influenced generations of fashion luminaries,

among them Nigerian designer Duro Olowu. 'A man always remembered women who wore Yves Saint Laurent, the clothes were extremely romantic and truly sexy', Olowu wrote in *Tank Magazine*. 'His African origins were very pronounced in his designs. Growing up in Africa, your first experience of a woman's appearance would be the flowing of fabric, the way it held and framed the female form. He took a typical tunic shape and recreated it in such an incredible way, and his use of rich Orientalist colours borrowed from the North African palette.'

Other designers of African descent have taken up Yves Saint Laurent's mantle. Morocco-born Alber Elbaz worked at Yves Saint Laurent Rive Gauche, Guy Laroche and Krizia, but it was his appointment as creative director of Lanvin in 2001 that propelled him to the status of fashion royalty thanks to his timeless, joyful designs. For Autumn/Winter 2010/11 Elbaz was inspired by a meeting with the UN held to discuss

potential projects for the brand in sub-Saharan Africa to come up with his idea of 'Africa in winter'. The collection featured dark dresses coated with feathers and amulet-like breastplates. He also supports African models, with Sudanese beauties Ajak Deng and Ataui Deng his most recent finds.

Tunisian Azzeline Alaïa established his brand in Paris in 1980 after stints at Christian Dior, Guy Laroche and Thierry Mugler and has been nicknamed the 'king of cling' for his signature body-conscious silhouettes. His collections have included python-skin dresses and footwear covered in cowrie shells, raffia and bells. Moroccan Joseph Ettedgui helped define luxury basics with his British brand Joseph, Tunisian Loris Azzaro's Paris-based label excels at showstopping gowns and fellow Tunisian Max Azria reigns over his BCBGMAXAZRIA global empire, which encompasses over 20 brands, including his eponymous line and Herve Leger.

INTO AFRICA

Throughout the decades, these and other international designers have created fashion's fantasies of the African aesthetic, cherry-picking from cultures, terrains and peoples. Thierry Mugler's African fetish culminated in his Spring/Summer 1985 show in which Iman walked with a monkey perched on her shoulder and a straw parasol held over her by a black male model in a thong. John Galliano's first haute couture collection for Christian Dior in 1997 included a series of silhouettes inspired by the East African tribes. Beaded hats, chokers and corsets were worn with long, silk evening gowns. Masai and Dinka warriors wear corsets but here Galliano crossed cultures with his use of the garment, which is more commonly regarded as originating from the 16th-century court of Henry II of France. Jean Paul Gaultier's 2005 haute couture show featured models baked in red mud and wearing Afro wigs, feathered dresses, shields made from tortoiseshell and a bridal gown consisting of a huge white leather African mask. In the same year, Bernhard Willhelm's Autumn/Winter 2005/06 menswear collection

refigured the boubou into gaudy, baggy streetwear covered in gold Africanised and animal prints.

The tribal trend reached a crescendo for Spring/Summer 2009. Alexander McQueen's kaleidoscopic prints hinted at savannah wildlife and landscapes. African fauna inspired Tsumori Chisato's feather dresses. Louis Vuitton teamed grass skirts with wooden accessories. Junya Watanabe's models wore towering headwear filled with sheaves of flowers. Vivienne Westwood tied and draped leopard- and zebra-print fabrics around the body. And Diane von Furstenberg, who has repeatedly returned to Africa in her collections since the 1970s, offered safari shirtdresses.

In 2010 Issey Miyake, Marc Jacobs, Kenzo, Gucci, Dries Van Noten and Eley Kishimoto all examined traditional textiles, in part due to the interest in Africa piqued by the 2010 FIFA World Cup in South Africa. Sports brands also followed suit with African-influenced lines. Puma collaborated with Nigerian-American artist Kehinde Wiley, who used African fabrics as a backdrop to his

portraits of football stars and as the basis of the prints in the collection.

Meanwhile Paul Smith paid homage to Italian photographer Daniel Tamagni's pictorial essay of La Sape (Société des Ambianceurs et Persons Élégants), a league of Congolese gentlemen known as 'sapeurs' who pray at the altar of designer fashion. The movement started in 1922 when G. A. Matsousa returned to the French colony from Paris dressed as a European aristocrat. Sapeurs in Brazzaville and Kinshasa now abide by a sartorial code of conduct that marks them out as local celebrities. Smith's collection brought the aesthetic full circle by feeding La Sape style back into high fashion.

For Autumn/Winter 2011/12 Walter Van Beirendonck used an all-black cast of models to show off his fringed menswear worn with tribal hoop accessories and make-up. Sass & Bide did feather-print caftan dresses. And Thakoon combined Masai colours with the costumes of Versailles to create bright plaids and paisleys and silhouettes with high-low hemlines.

Left to right: Jean Paul Gaultier, Spring/Summer 2005 haute couture collection; Junya Watanabe,

Spring/Summer 2009 ready-to-wear collection; Suno Resort collection, 2011

*Left: Paul Smith,
Spring/Summer
2010 collection*

*Right: Sapeur
Willy Covary*

It's those designers who collaborate with African artisans in order to harness authentic materials and techniques, and bridge the gap between African-born and African-inspired by basing socially responsible production on the continent, who create the most meaningful results. Ethiopian model, actress and philanthropist Liya Kebede aims to help Ethiopian weavers with LemLem. Her line of children's and womenswear is hand-spun and embroidered in Addis Ababa and sold worldwide. Edun, which was established by Ali Hewson and her husband Bono and is part-owned by luxury group LVMH, is a similar 'trade not aid' initiative. The line is produced mainly in East Africa and its profits go to sustainable farming communities in Uganda, and to funding children in Kibera, the largest slum in Kenya.

Likewise, Suno was established by New Yorkers Max Osterweis and Erin Beatty as a response to Kenya's post-election turmoil in 2008. The pair went to Nairobi, where they used Osterweis's vast collection of vintage Kenyan kangas (colourful cloth with aphorisms printed on them) to create the brand's first collection for Spring/Summer 2009. 'I wanted to create jobs in Kenya, elevate the cloth and build a print-driven brand

with an essence of optimism', he says. Suno now shows during New York Fashion Week, creates its own kanga-inspired prints and employs up to 130 Kenyan tailors. 'Already other designers are asking us about working out of Kenya. Suno speaks of Africa as a place to get things done, and as a source of inspiration.'

African designers have mixed feelings about the ways in which Western designers adopt the visual language of Africa. While it keeps the continent in style, clichés are inevitable. 'European designers choose certain colours or materials without necessarily understanding their value. Now African designers have begun to be recognised for using their heritage in a way that contributes to the evolution of their culture by creating contemporary versions of their traditional crafts', says Sudanese designer Omer Asim. 'This is more interesting because it is relevant to young urban Africans who want to wear things that express their identity and also gives the diaspora a means of connecting with their homeland in a more authentic way.'

British/Ghanaian designer Joe Casely-Hayford is unsurprised by Africa's continued influence on global

fashion but sees its intelligent application as a positive thing. 'Designers and artists are drawn to the unique vitality and purity of Africa and the prominence of the free spirit, which is sadly often found missing from our day to day lives. Today's most influential designers have a global appeal while retaining an indigenous handwriting.'

This approach reflects the way in which African people have always combined cultures in their dress, a practice that contemporary African designers, working to international fashion seasons, have accelerated. They move beyond what is perceived to be the African aesthetic by embracing genuine fabrics and styles of dress yet looking to the rest of the world for inspiration. The fashion world is going global and the African influence has gone beyond a trend to become part of the fashion lexicon. The best design is no longer defined by its borders, yet recognises where it came from. It delivers desirable, inspirational pieces stemming from an open-minded environment, whether that's in Luanda or London, Maputo or Milan, Nairobi or New York. The future holds joint partnerships and a level playing field that is not defined by destination.

IT'S A JUNGLE IN HERE

The rise of African fashion is inextricably linked to its models and muses. In 1975 Iman Mohamed Abdulmajid was presented to New York's fashion scene at a press conference tabled by photographer Peter Beard. He claimed that she was an illiterate tribeswoman whom he'd discovered herding cattle on the Saharan plains. In reality Iman was born in Somalia, the daughter of a diplomat and a gynaecologist, and spoke five languages. She had met Beard while studying at the University of Nairobi and was an accomplice in his mythologising scheme for three months. It worked: her first modelling assignment was for *Vogue*, she became an Yves Saint Laurent muse, and she remains one of the most successful African models of all time.

Paco Rabanne and Yves Saint Laurent were among the first designers to use models of colour in the 1960s, the decade in which Ugandan princess Elizabeth of Toro and African-Americans Naomi Sims and Donyale Luna became the first black magazine cover-girls. Beverly Johnson was the first black woman to be on the cover of *Vogue* in the 1970s. It was also in the 1970s and 1980s that the catwalks of New York, London, Milan and Paris belonged to black girls. Africans Iman, Rebecca Ayoko, Khadija Adam, Katoucha Niane, Amina Warsuma and Jinnie Tuomba joined Jamaican Grace Jones and African-Americans Sandi Bass, Pat Cleveland, Peggy Dillard, Billie Blair, Toukie Smith and Bethann Hardison in working for pro-black fashion houses such as Pierre Cardin, Courrèges, Stephen Burrows, Oscar de la Renta, Thierry Mugler, Givenchy and Halston.

'It was a unique time. We were following the yellow brick road and didn't even realise it. It was all brand new and it became our moment', remembers Hardison, who set up her own model agency, Bethann Management, in 1984, and helped make Tyson Beckford's career. She also formed the Black Girls Coalition with Iman in 1988 as a means of championing models of colour.

When she witnessed the decline in popularity of black and African models throughout the 1990s and early 2000s, she was driven to speak up. 'There were only a handful of African girls you could recognise, all the older girls were disappearing and hardly any new ones were replacing them.'

Exceptions to the rule include Alek Wek, Waris Darie, Kiara Kabakuru and Anna Getaneh. Hardison took action against fashion's whitewash in 2007 by hosting the first in a series of 'town hall' meetings in New York that challenged the industry's lack of diversity. The effects were felt immediately. The following seasons saw more black girls on the catwalks and in 2008 *Vogue Italia*'s editor in chief Franca Sozzani instigated the first all-black issue, which sold out twice over. Hardison helped cast models for the issue and has gone on to contribute to the *Vogue Black* website, where she profiles the growing swell of African girls such as Ajak Deng, Aminata Niaria and Georgie Baddiel. 'Give me

anybody who has a touch of jungle fever, I've got their back. Sozzani understands that we all go into society's melting pot. Since 2007 so much has changed but we still have to keep our eye on the ball.'

'When Alek Wek came on to the scene in 1995 she was called the real African beauty. In the fashion industry there was only room for one black supermodel at a time', says Anna Getaneh, who these days runs the Ethiopian Children's Fund and the Johannesburg-based fashion enterprise African Mosaique. 'So to have several African beauties with different looks working now is refreshing. It's positive for Africa and also encourages aspiring models on the continent.'

Inspired by the crossover success of models such as Liya Kebede, Flaviana Matata, Honorine Uwera, Kinée Diouf, Agbani Darego, Ajuma Nasenyana and Ubah Hassan, the hunt is on to find new beauty on the continent. The major modelling agencies have African scouts. Elite Model Look has extended the global

Iman, one of Africa's most successful models

Model Aminata Niaria

modelling competition to several African countries and South African TV network M-Net hosts an annual continent-wide search, *Face of Africa*. Oluchi Onweagba was the first winner in 1998 and remains its most successful export to date. And as the fashion industry burgeons across Africa, modelling is becoming a viable career choice for many.

Fashion weeks are multiplying fast. FAFA in Kenya, Mozambique Fashion Week, Swahili Fashion Week in Tanzania, Fashion Business Angola, Casablanca Fashion Week and Zimbabwe Fashion Week are just a handful of them. *ARISE* magazine hosts shows in London, New York and Paris as well as its own fashion week in Lagos. And African diaspora fashion weeks have also cropped up in New York, London and Dublin.

South Africa undoubtedly holds the best prospects for models, with numerous fashion weeks held throughout the year. Dr Precious Motsepe established African Fashion International (AFI) in 2006, which now

produces Cape Town Fashion Week, Joburg Fashion Week and Africa Fashion Week. Tanzanian model Millen Magese is a mainstay of AFI events. 'Our aim is to provide a platform from which African designers and models can launch international careers', says Motsepe. 'Ours is a land of diversity, a reality that is beautifully translated into our fashion. We can't help but be noticed within an industry that is always looking for fresh talent.'

GENERATION NOW

The success of the new generation of designers, models and fashion scenes around Africa is a reflection of Africa's success as a whole. The continent is gradually emerging as a global power thanks to increased trade and investment between Africa and the rest of the world and improved political stability and economic growth in burgeoning democracies such as Nigeria, South

Africa, Kenya, Botswana and Ghana. According to a 2011 study by the African Development Bank, one in three Africans (313 million people) is now defined as middle class. Growing numbers are well-educated, well-travelled, living in urban areas and helping to drive future economic and cultural development.

Booming manufacturing, finance, corporate and technology sectors are being rivalled by the creative industries and big business and governments are beginning to take note. The fashion and textile industry is a significant contributor to the GDP of many countries. In South Africa, it typically employs 200,000 people and generates over R20 billion (US$2.9 billion) per annum. By working on a small scale and using local labour and resources, it's creating jobs, keeping traditional craftsmanship alive, developing fair trade networks, bolstering retail and building a business model that benefits the African economy from the ground up.

African fashion is also being aided by a rapid increase in telecommunications. Due to improved cable and satellite connectivity, Africa now has more than 500 million mobile phone users, 110 million internet users and 25 million Facebook members. This allows for e-commerce, new media and social media to connect designers quickly, easily and cheaply to their customers and each other. Blogspot and Twitter both rank in the top 10 most visited sites in Nigeria, Kenya and South Africa, with fashion taking up no small part in the conversation. African and diaspora portals such as BellaNaija, Fashizblack, iFashion, HauteFashion, Ladybrille, African Style Daily, Style House Files, One Nigerian Boy and Shadders and e-commerce sites including My Asho, Heritage 360 and Agnes and Lola all transport African fashion to the world.

There has been a surge in African fashion periodicals too. While Condé Nast stirred up much debate by passing on the option of bringing out a *Vogue Africa* in 2010, African glossies such as *Canoe*, *Fab*, *Pop'Africana*, *Clam*, *True Love*, *African Woman*, *Thisday Style* and *ARISE* are all read by opinion-formers in search of quality African fashion editorials. *ARISE* chairman and editor in chief Nduka Obaigbena says: '*ARISE* magazine is leading the way in satisfying unprecedented demand for Africa's finest designers. We're here to show the world that Africa is at the cutting edge of international fashion.'

Designers have both the means and the channels of communication to achieve recognition. They are grounded in traditions but are exposed to international trends and tastes, allowing them to satisfy local demand, attract international interest and shape contemporary African identities. It's this axis of influences and agendas that is making African fashion so exciting and vital right now.

CHALLENGING TIMES

The road ahead isn't an easy one, however. The difficulties facing African fashion's growth remain real. For example, there is a lack of formal fashion educational facilities, which creates weaknesses in all aspects of the industry from pattern-cutting and styling to marketing and PR. There is no continent-wide official body to unify and encourage funding for designers. And poor infrastructure in most countries means that frequent power cuts, lack of equipment and unreliable transportation pushes up costs. Designers can struggle to produce small orders to high standards within the timeframe and price points required to fulfil seasonal overseas orders.

The second-hand clothes market is a hot topic in Kenya, Zambia, Ghana, Tunisia, Zimbabwe, Rwanda and Senegal, where a significant proportion of donations to charities in the USA and Europe ends up. Their import, distribution, repair and resale has become a thriving industry and provides consumers with access to affordable fashion. In Kenya fashion-conscious shoppers use dressing agents who hand-pick the best items from each shipment before it even reaches the mitumba markets. The trade creates employment and choice, but at the expense of local designers who can't compete on price. Increasingly cheap imports of new clothing from Asia compound the problem. 'Second-hand clothes sellers are a necessary evil here but as Kenyan brands come in and create more stable employment, they can pull from a pool of talent who have trained themselves in becoming merchandisers and salesmen', says Jeffrey Kimathi of Nairobi-based streetwear brand Jamhuri Wear.

Some countries have tackled the issue by banning the import of fashion and textiles, or taxing them heavily in an attempt to stimulate local production, but this approach creates different issues. In Nigeria textile imports were outlawed in 2003, which resulted in a large number of manufacturing companies closing down and a rise in black-market imports. Although restrictions were somewhat lifted in 2010, the lack of choice of fabrics and factories remains an ongoing problem for designers.

But according to Lagos-based designer Folake Folarin-Coker of Tiffany Amber, creativity conquers all on a continent that has had more than its fair share of strife. 'It's true, there is still a lack of infrastructure, fabrics, technical know-how and government support. But these constraints only make us super resourceful and as more people train as fashion designers, it is becoming a domino effect. It's been a long process but now we're ready to compete. The future of African fashion is in the hands of great designers.'

Dress by Tiffany Amber

FASHION

DURO
OLOWU

Prints
Charming

At Duro Olowu's New York Fashion Week debut at the Milk Studios, his models, including Georgie Baddiel, Kinée Diouf and Sigail Currie, came into view wearing an elegant cacophony of colours, prints, fabrics and textures. Velvet, printed silks, vintage textiles, merino jacquard wool and Linton tweed were patchworked, layered, reassembled and panelled together to create sweeping floor-length, bias-cut dresses, fitted zip-up blazers, multi-peplum jackets, wide-legged cropped trousers and bell-sleeved cocoon cardigans. The look was in equal part noble, womanly and cosy.

'My intention was to create a freestyle, chic wardrobe for an independent spirit', says Olowu, who cites South American gauchos, Mexican screen icon María Félix and African-American Harlem Renaissance photographer James Van Der Zee as the touchstones of the Autumn/Winter 2011/12 collection.

Married to Thelma Golden, chief curator of The Studio Museum in Harlem, and with customers including Michelle Obama, Iman, Bethann Hardison, Shala Monroque and Iris Apfel, it's little wonder Olowu made the move to New York after several seasons at London Fashion Week. But his story begins elsewhere: in Lagos, where he was born and raised. 'I was a child of the 1970s, I saw the world from the cushion on the floor and I always drew. Lagos was a bustling city, I loved the way people always made an effort in how they dressed. Nigerian clothes look very structured but are actually very light. It's all about posture and mixing fabrics and prints. My mother had a very carefree style, she'd wear a Gucci scarf with a skirt made by a local tailor. It has all became part of my aesthetic.'

Olowu trained as a lawyer in London but, moved by Yves Saint Laurent's vision of 'attainable beauty', he started the label Olowu Golding with his first wife Elaine Golding in the mid-1990s. After the marriage ended, he began his eponymous line for Spring/Summer 2004 and opened a boutique on Portobello Road, selling a capsule collection of voluminous empire-line dresses based on the Yoruba boubou. 'It was a very joyful, effortless and comfortable dress. It had a deep V neckline, long sleeves and was made from viscose georgette so it flowed nicely when you walked. If you were in Paris, London or Lagos, you could have worn that dress, day or night.'

In 2005 US *Vogue* featured it, thus beginning a craze for what became known as the 'Duro Dress'. He won New Designer of the Year at the British Fashion Awards (the first brand to do so without having done a catwalk show) and gained stockists around the world, among them Barneys New York and Maria Louisa, Paris.

He's since collected numerous accolades, including International Designer of the Year at the 2010 Africa Fashion Week Awards, and opened a new boutique in St James's, central London. His loyal customers flock to this intimate space to graze on his instinctual union of reclaimed couture fabrics with his own kaleidoscopic prints, and talent for form-flattering tailoring and bohemian draping. His handcrafted, limited-edition pieces are ageless, sensual and above all celebrate the urbane woman. 'I thrive on authenticity without being precious and want to make things that last', he says. 'You don't have to be a size zero, or rich, to look good. I hope my clothes champion women and inspire them to feel dignified, confident and sexy.'

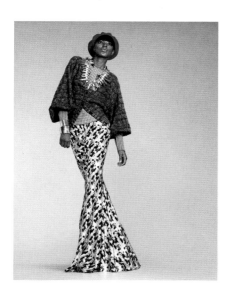

Olowu's Autumn/Winter 2011/12 collection is a cacophony of prints, fabrics and textures and exposes his talent for form-flattering tailoring and bohemian draping.

For over 20 years Malian designer Lamine Badian Kouyaté has been a rebellious force in Parisian fashion. An upcycling frontrunner, his streetwise designs are functional, thoughtful, liberating and celebratory in equal measure and, above all, are like no others.

Born in 1962 in Bamako, he grew up customising second-hand clothes found in local markets and visiting local tailors. He studied art in Dakar and architecture in Strasbourg and Paris, where in 1989 he started Xuly Bët Funkin' Fashion Factory (*xuly bët* means 'keep an open mind' or 'watch out' in Wolof). This time around, he scoured flea markets as much out of necessity as a statement of intent. 'In Africa second-hand clothing is *passage obligé* for the people, it's all they can afford. In the West we throw it all away, it's too much waste, so I decided to do something with it. Fashion is itself a cycle, after all.'

He took discarded clothes and recreated them in ways that emphasised the journey of the cloth – from a scarf to a skirt or a jacket to a dress, and from the rubbish bin to the high-fashion boutique. While used clothes from the West are dumped in Africa, Kouyaté turned the tables on the home of haute couture to prove that appropriation was in fact a two-way street. Visible red stitching and signs of repair, brash screen-printed logos and skin-tight silhouettes that idolised the body beneath became his calling card and acted as his implicit comment on Africa's interaction with the world.

XULY BËT

Recycling Pioneer

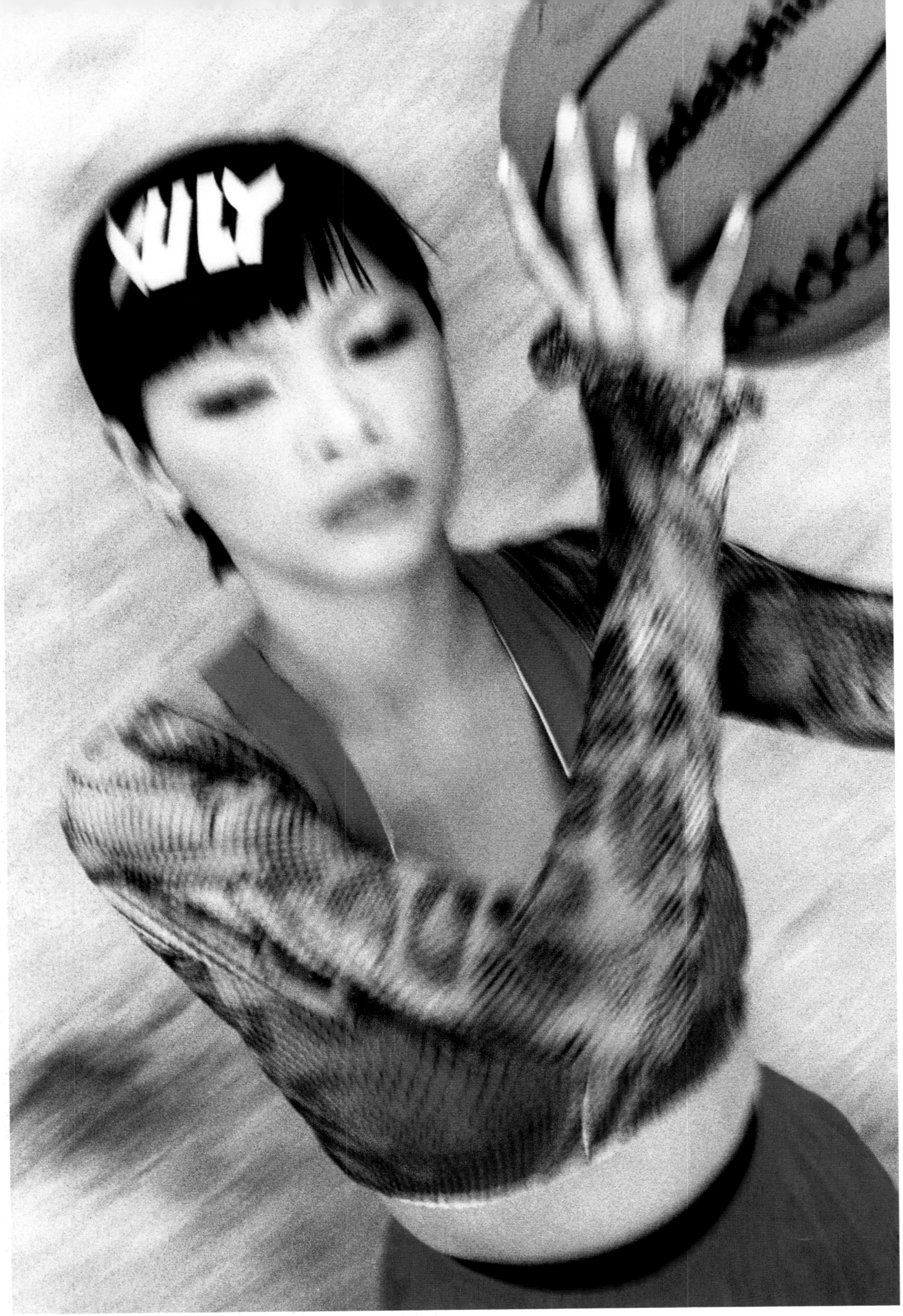

Kouyaté presented his first catwalk collection in 1993 in Paris, was awarded the prestigious Creator of the Year award in 1994 by the *New York Times* and received the ANDAM award in 1996 from the French Ministry of Culture and the Chambres Syndicale de la Couture Parisienne. He's exhibited at the MoMu Fashion Museum, Antwerp, the Victoria & Albert Museum, London, and the Grimaldi Forum, Monaco, and taken part in fashion events across five continents. Kouyaté has also collaborated with brands such as 3 Suisses and Puma and dressed musicians including INXS, Neneh Cherry, Keziah Jones, Soul II Soul and Grace Jones, who walked for him at New York Fashion Week in 2009. 'There have been so many highs, I have a reservoir of experiences, but Grace has always been one of my major influences. I could design with her in mind for the rest of my life.'

Today his collections may be less distressed, but his anti-elitist vision and instinctive way of working remains the same. He eschews trends and themes or even commercial concerns, and instead concentrates on empowering the African woman. 'I hone in on women's lives and how one of my suits or a dresses can work for them. Fashion is not about the designer's ego, it's about putting heart and energy into building a space for females to move in', he says. 'The woman's condition in Africa has made major advances but there are still so many barriers to break. I want to bring light to the history of Africa and project a united future.'

At Africa Fashion Week 2010 Xuly Bët showed an all-black collection of hooded and figure-hugging dresses in leather, Lurex, sequins and denim.

MIMI PLANGE

Afro-disiac

Mimi Plange had a eureka moment in February 2011. After several seasons of showing at New York Fashion Week as Boudoir D'huîtres, her first eponymous show for Autumn/Winter 2011/12 was given the seal of approval by both established Nigerian designer Duro Olowu and US *Vogue*'s André Leon Talley, who helped Plange edit the presentation.

She examined Christiana Oware Knudsen's book *The Patterned Skin*, a study of ethnic scarification in Plange's native Ghana, to come up with a collection called Scarred Perfection that was full of billowing pleating, elaborate stitching and ornamentation. Dresses were key – blood-red gabardine sheaths, hot pink silk bustier cocktail dresses and bejewelled floor-length crepe silk gowns oozed elegance, while black leather biker trousers, beige mohair capes and white wool T-shirts were all wearable, tough girl must-haves.

'Before clothing, many Africans would scar their faces and bodies with patterns and symbols as a method of tribal identification. It's a very painful process that shocks some people but beauty is in the eye of the beholder', says Plange, whose mother (a former *Drum* magazine model) has one such scar on her cheek. 'I am motivated by those things that make us question how we represent ourselves to other people.'

Plange was born in Accra and moved to California with her family as a child. She studied architecture and fashion before relocating to New York, where she worked for both Patricia Fields and Rachel Roy. She launched Boudoir D'huîtres in 2007 with her business partner Ibrahim Ndoye and the label has become known for staying true to her twin influences: Victorian fashion and her African heritage. 'They may seem like opposing forces but both have an old-world sense of craftsmanship and individuality. I translate these themes in a luxurious, up-to-date way.' Her Autumn/Winter 2009/10 collection joined Mozart's Queen of the Night with Egyptian mysticism while her safari-ready Spring/Summer 2011 looks stemmed from her trip to South Africa, where she showed at Africa Fashion Week. 'Fashion is fantasy, it makes us dream big dreams and that's what Africa needs right now.'

Two of a Kind

CASELY-HAYFORD

Joe Casely-Hayford's grandfather Joseph Ephraim Casely-Hayford MBE (1866–1930), the prominent Cape Coast author, lawyer, Cambridge scholar and pan-African thinker, based his novel *Ethiopia Unbound* around the concept of a double consciousness brought about by having two places of origin, of belonging both to Africa and to its colonial rulers. This notion of 'twoness' survives in the menswear brand Joe runs with his son Charlie. 'Themes of clashing cultures are central to our output. Being British-born we're enthralled by duality and the crossing points of ethnicity, which imbues our collection with a subliminal wash of African style', Joe explains.

He first trained as a tailor, then attended London's Central Saint Martins and went into business in the early 1980s. He made stage costumes for musicians including The Clash, Lou Reed and U2 as well as for ballet and film productions. He showed in Paris, London and Tokyo and stocked his men's and womenswear worldwide. And between 2005 and 2008 he was creative director of Gieves & Hawkes. 'I had always been considered an anti-establishment designer so it was an appealing challenge for me to contemporise such a bastion of English tailoring.' During his tenure he received an OBE, and the Casely-Hayfords were voted the most influential family in Britain by the Black Power List.

Charlie was born in 1986 and studied art at Central Saint Martins and The Courtauld Institute of Art. He worked for magazines and galleries and as a model before launching Casely-Hayford with his father in 2008. Their early collection began their conversation about duality, whether in the function of the clothing, the polarity of their references or in the very nature of their double act.

Spring/Summer 2010 has been their most overtly African collection to date. Joe and Charlie have stolen elements from the myriad subcultures that coexist in east London (artists, rude boys, indie kids and Turkish immigrants) to create a dangerously new style they call 'Afro punk'. Sports fabrics were turned into tailored suits, Ottoman and Wedgwood prints covered baggy trousers, silver chains buttoned onto shirt collars and multiple scarves formed 'hankersleeves' – an allusion to the hooped adornments some African tribes use to elongate limbs.

'For young black people born in the West there are many alternatives to the hip hop lifestyle that dominates black youth culture. We can enjoy a broader cultural awareness without imposing limitations on ourselves. Afro punk is the sartorial manifestation of being globally aware in the 21st century', says Joe. 'I call my peers kleptomaniacs because they draw from different identities', adds Charlie. 'A lot of the ideas I come up with my father's already done 20 years ago. But today it means something different because of the social context. The dichotomy between us always creates interesting results.'

The father and son duo explore clashing cultures and nomadic lifestyles to create a dangerous new style called 'Afro punk.'

Recent collections continue to walk the tightrope between innovation and tradition via the cultural nomad, specifically desert-dwellers in the case of Spring/Summer 2011. 'We were interested in the tranquil energy of the Bedouin tribe as a symbol of something real and minimal that negates the excess so prevalent during the last decade', says Joe. Drawstring linen trousers, washed-out safari jackets and panama cotton collarless shirts in sand, stone and greige are both fragile and camouflaging, lightweight and protective. 'Each season we present a different facet of the same man. Our intent is to create desirable, enduring and understated clothing that tells a story.'

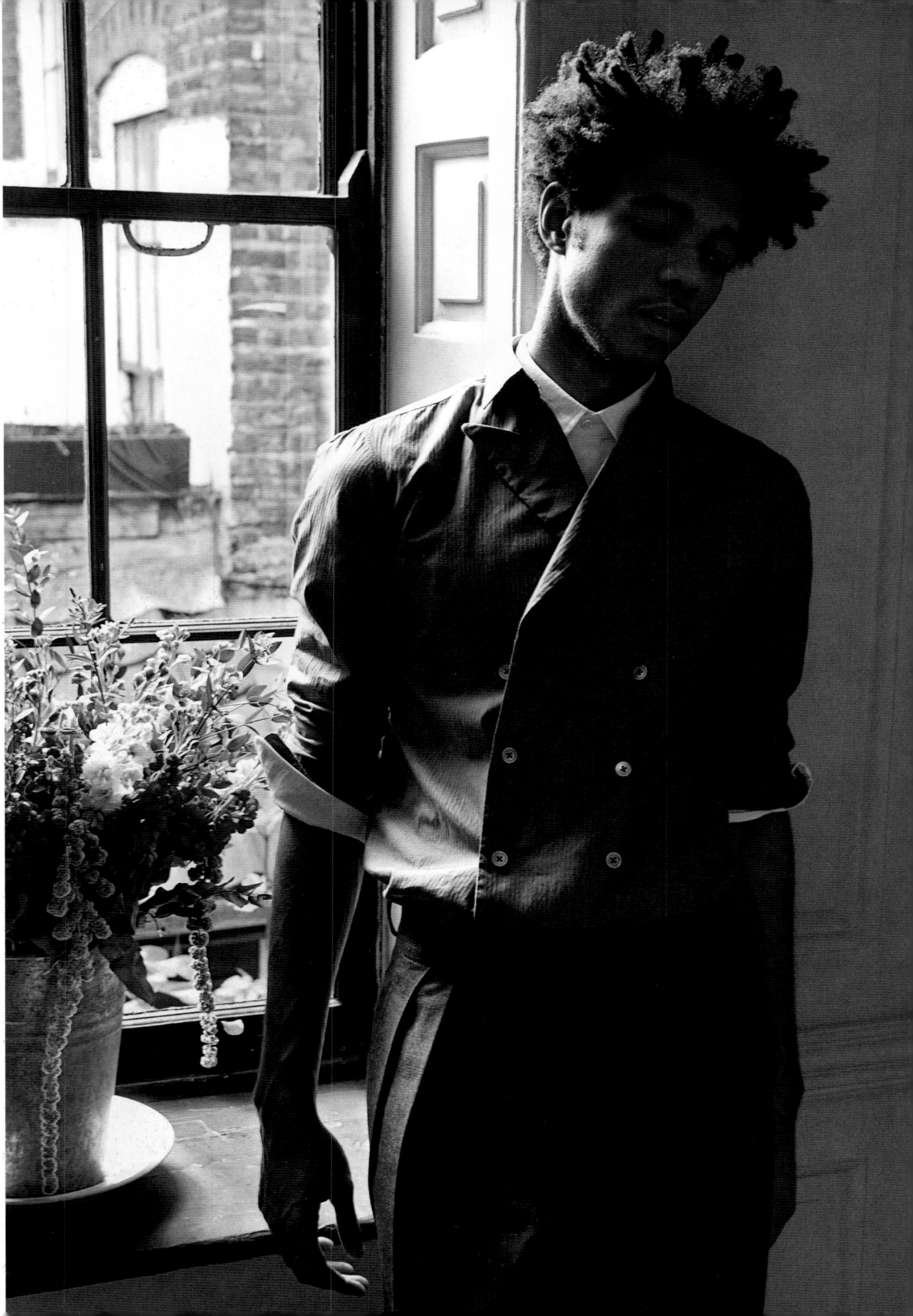

'Our intent is to create desirable, enduring and understated clothing that tells a story.'

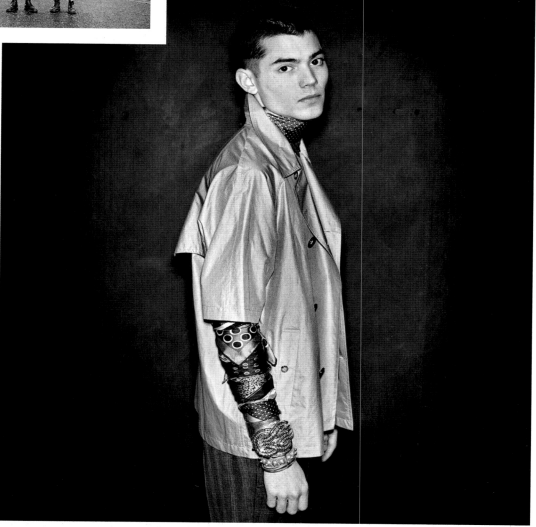

FAFA

Destination Nairobi

In the wake of the violent unrest and ethnic tension that shook Kenya as a result of the December 2007 presidential elections, local designer Ann McCreath of Afrocentric brand KikoRomeo decided to establish an event that would promote peace. Held in Nairobi National Park in May 2008, the Festival for African Fashion and Arts (FAFA) brought over 1,000 guests and 13 designers together for a catwalk show that was the first of its kind.

'Everyone was united in the desire to do something positive for the country and the show's energy was mind-blowing', McCreath recalls. 'FAFA is about artists in society opening the minds of citizens to different cultures and ideas. Kenya is made up of over 40 communities, each with its own identity. Focusing on the positives of diversity, through creativity and glamour, FAFA unites people.' It has now become an annual celebration of fashion, music and the arts and has grown in size and ambition to include fashion workshops and a second day for emerging talent.

Designers from across Africa, such as Nigeria's Tiffany Amber, Senegal's Mame Faguèye Bâ, Tanzania's Mustafa Hassanali, Ghana's Kofi Ansah, Ethiopia's African Mosaique, Uganda's Arapapa, Zanzibar's Doreen Mashika and South Africa's Thula Sindi have come to FAFA. They've joined local designers such as Kooroo, John Kaveke, Betty Vanetti, Monica Kanari, Moo Cow, Deepa Dosaja, Le Collane di Betta and Patricia Mbela. 'African fashion is as varied as the continent itself so we wanted to include designers from several countries and embrace different concepts of dress', adds McCreath. 'We've had a big impact and we're well on our way to realising our ambition to create a world-class, internationally recognised festival on Kenyan soil.'

KOOROO

Hebret Lakew hails from Addis Ababa and studied fashion in New York, where she also worked for MaxMara. Enid Lanez was born in Uganda and travelled extensively prior to the pair meeting in Nairobi in 2003. Kooroo (meaning 'be proud' in Amharic) concentrates on harnessing sustainable materials and production to create easy, flattering womenswear. They've shown in Edinburgh and Dar es Salaam and at FAFA. Spring/Summer 2011 offered linen swing coats, bias-cut dresses and slouchy trousers in sand, stone, bronze and orange with ostrich-shell beading on belts and necklines. 'FAFA has created a platform for designers to show the world their creativity in a positive light. It's important for designers throughout Africa to work together to strengthen the fashion scene. We hope to do our part by creating local employment and bringing an ethnic fusion to our designs.'

JOHN KAVEKE

Mombasa-born Kaveke studied fashion in Nairobi and
Barcelona and worked in textile design and teaching prior to
launching his label in 2000. He's twice taken part in M-Net
Face of Africa and shown in Nigeria, Bosnia and Ethiopia as
well as at FAFA. 'I want people to think of Kenya when they
think of John Kaveke. Living in a country that is known for its
scenery, its mix of African, Asian and European cultures and
its indigenous craftsmanship is a great source of inspiration.'
He works with Masai women in Kiserian for his beading and
combines kikoi and kanga with leather, denim, silk and linen
to create his theatrical men's and women's collections. For
Spring/Summer 2011 he cited 18th-century men's coats, punk
and lingerie to come up with a strongly tailored, androgynous
collection in deep reds and browns.

The slogan T-shirt has a long and illustrious history as a means of social commentary. Vivienne Westwood's Destroy and God Save the Queen T-shirts arguably kick-started it all in the 1970s. Katharine Hamnett's ethical messages in the 1980s urged us to Choose Life, while Henry Holland's 2006 Fashion Groupies collection – Cause Me Pain Hedi Slimane, Get Yer Freak On Giles Deacon – took the trend to tongue-and-cheek extremes. More recently Kenyan sports brand Jamhuri Wear caused a craze in New York with its clever spin on the tourist I Heart NY T-shirts, replacing the heart with a map of Africa. And Ghanaian brand Kayobi Clothing said it all with Make Fufu Not War.

Loud Speaker
GLORIA WAVAMUNNO

Ugandan designer Gloria Wavamunno also got it all off her chest during her Autumn/Winter 2011/12 London Fashion Week show. One white T-shirt screamed I'm Responsible For My Africa while another had the words Live Aid crossed out and the word Trade printed underneath. 'I am in love with my continent at the moment. My art is Ugandan, it's African, and I am extremely proud of where I come from', she explains. Her Not a Dream, My Soulmate collection was otherwise stylistically less confrontational with cute blazers made from Ugandan bark cloth worn with bustiers, full pleated skirts, hot pants and cropped trousers in shades of gold, black and blue.

Wavamunno was born in London in 1985, where her parents had relocated in order to escape civil war, but the family moved back to Uganda shortly after her birth as peace returned under President Yoweri Museveni. Wavamunno's mother was her first fashion icon. 'I would see this glow and confidence flow from her as she dressed herself. This is where my fascination with the spirit behind clothes and the emotion they evoke in the wearer began.'

She studied fine art at the American InterContinental University in London and interned at Ozwald Boateng before launching her label in Kampala in early 2009 with a collection called L.O.V.E. She's since opened a boutique, shown twice at African Fashion Week in Johannesburg and developed signature looks that include 1980s-inspired cocktail dresses, jumpsuits and harem pants in African prints. Feathers, frills, shoulder pads, unisex bowties and sweetheart necklines all add sugar and spice to her effervescent, power-dressing womenswear.

Music and fashion are inextricably linked in the work of Moroccan designer Amine Bendriouich. 'Music is very important to my creative process. I can't spend a day without it. For me it's about finding alternative means of expression because designing clothing is limited', he says. 'Fashion is the result of the people I meet, the places I go and the music I hear.' Describing his aesthetic as a cross between *ayobaness* (South African township slang for 'cool') and rock and roll, his unconventional attitude has always got him noticed.

Bendriouich grew up in Marrakech sketching fantasy wardrobes for himself and his girlfriends. He studied fashion in Tunisia and moved to Casablanca in 2007 to work for a textile company. At the same time he started a T-shirt line called Stounami, which caused a stir in Arabic society for its defiant slogans, and enabled him to establish both his brand ABCB (Amine Bendriouich Couture & Bullshit) and Contemporary Moroccan Roots, an event that brings fashion, photography, film and music together to create a platform for Morocco's new cultural landscape.

In 2009 he was the only African finalist in the Goethe-Institut's Createurope fashion competition, and was granted the use of a flat, showroom and workshop in Berlin for one year. He's remained there ever since but his production is still based back home. 'Morocco has no fashion scene as we know it in Europe, but I want to build a bridge between the two places. Love, peace and difference!'

Bendriouich's unisex, deconstructed tailoring is based as often on Moroccan clothing such as sarouels and djelabbahs as on hip hop streetwear. The results find a positive synergy between hedonism and tradition. 'Since King Mohammad VI's ascension [1999] there has been more freedom of artistic expression. We now have Casablanca Fashion Week and young designers are beginning to realise that clothes can go beyond the caftan. The balance is changing and the future of Moroccan fashion is going to be very interesting indeed.'

Medina
Maverick

AMINE BENDRIOUICH

One of the new breed
taking Moroccan fashion
way beyond the realm of
caftan chic.

MAKI OH

The Thinker

With her label Maki Oh, Amaka Osakwe challenges prevailing notions of beauty by delving into African cultures to create intricately constructed conversation pieces that embody the principles of preservation, strength and individuality. The seduction of Maki Oh is in its unison of emotion, intuition, belonging and sexual energy that goes beyond conventional ideas of what constitutes pretty clothes.

Brought up in Lagos, Osakwe studied fashion at the Arts University College at Bournemouth, UK, and returned home to launch her label with Autumn/Winter 2010/11's Everything In Proportion. It took as its reference the Dipo rite of passage ceremony of rural Ghana, a three-week process during which young females shed the vestiges of their childhoods and are ornately adorned with beads and garments while remaining partly naked. The final Klama dance announces the arrival of womanhood.

Her collection cloaked the body in outfits that likewise simultaneously covered and revealed. Sheer tops were embellished with a calabash jigsaw (an update of Oumou Sy and Anggy Haif's calabash bikinis from the 1990s). Adire was turned into voluminous shorts and miniskirts. Baggy trousers suggestive of agbada were made from antique silk, and jersey dresses were overlaid with chiffon and stiffened with eko-painted symbols suggestive of the intimate female physique beneath.

'I liken the collection to my own coming of age through fashion', Osakwe says. 'I wanted to make Nigerians aware of their own handmade fabrics and explored both couture sewing techniques and the tailoring and embroidery of men's traditional clothing. But I'm most inspired by adire – its marvellous indigo dyes and proverbs behind different motifs, which are handed down through generations. The collection is infused with hidden meanings and secret conversations.'

Maki Oh was among a collective of designers who celebrated Nigeria's 2010 Golden Jubilee by donating outfits to a charity collection in association with Lagos boutique Temple Muse. Her six-piece outfit assembled a Nigerian national dress by drawing on garments worn by different tribes and was dedicated to women who have changed society since independence. The wrapper skirt symbolised the dulcet tones of jazz singer Frances Kuboye. Women's rights activist Funmilayo Anikulapo-Kuti inspired the cropped top with an ase-oke pouch. Malaria researcher Ify Aniebo's net shawl serves as a shelter for the wearer. And the adire headpiece embodied artist Nike Davies Okundaye's promotion of female empowerment through textiles.

Autumn/Winter 2011/12 was driven by an interpretation of classical pianist Ludovico Einaudi's composition 'Love is a Mystery', with each look acting as a chapter in the story of a girl who falls in and out of love. Osakwe covered silk adire and mesh in shredded sleeping mats, intricate neon yellow embroidery and silver fringing made from unravelled ase-oke. Shapes were sometimes restrictive (button-down shirts and one-legged jumpsuits) and sometimes loose (T-shirt dresses and pantaloons with garters).

'Everything's been done before, they say, but there's still so much about Africa to be explored.'

'Sleeping mats are traditionally presented to brides on their wedding day. The pakiti adire motif used in this collection translates as "May you lie on this mat and have many children." So I've used the actual mat, and the print, and invented my own colours of love. The collection begins with "level-headed grey", which radiates through to bordeaux and indigo and at the point where she's totally in love it's acid yellow. When she is battling against love, the silhouette becomes strict but the fabrics become transparent so as to show that she's still open.'

The collection earned her the Emerging Designer award at *ARISE* Magazine Fashion Week – Lagos 2011 but she's far from resting on her laurels yet. 'Living in the hub of a culture I adore is what motivates me. Everything's been done before they say, but there's still so much about Africa to be explored. The real work starts here and now.'

Maki Oh's 'national dress', part of Temple Muse's La Dame La Muse collection, is dedicated to six women who have made a positive impact on society since Nigeria's independence. When not worn, the one-off outfit fits on a wooden map of Nigeria.

ERIC RAISINA

Spiritual
Explorer

Eric Raisina possesses a gentle soul and a delicate touch.
Renowned for his feather-soft, handwoven textiles that
seemingly beg to be stroked, his fate has always been wedded to
bringing beauty into the world. He was born in Antananarivo,
Madagascar, in 1969 and spent his childhood exploring the
island's lush flora and fauna. 'I used to sketch everything
around me, especially landscapes', he recalls. 'And as a teenager
I fell deeply in love with Malagasy silk, raffia and cotton and
learnt how to crochet and embroider.'

In 1990 a collage dress he made from Malagasy paper for
his sister to wear in a beauty pageant caused a sensation.
Encouraged, he pursued his 'atelier clandestine' and two years
later took part in Antananarivo's annual fashion festival. His
collection took first prize and earned him a scholarship to the
École Duperré in Paris. 'I enjoyed five years full of encounters
in a haven for creativity. I discovered so many disciplines and
would spend my evenings at the Centre Pompidou.'

Raisina did a masters at the Institut Français de la Mode, where he fully developed his handwoven fabrics. For stimulation, he travelled to Cambodia in 1996. 'I'd heard about the silk fabrics made there, and about the temples. When I arrived I was amazed by the similarities between Malagasy and Cambodian people and found a spirituality and energy there that I'd never felt before in my life. I got a summer job at a silk farm in Angkor and then set up my own workshop.' While still a student, his silk and raffia fabrics attracted the French couture houses. He produced one-off pieces for Christian Lacroix and Christian Dior, and Yves Saint Laurent's muse Loulou de la Falaise commissioned him to develop a silk-fringed ribbon for lining coats that he's since coined 'silk fur'.

He debuted his Haute Texture line at the International Festival of African Fashion (FIMA) in Niger in 1998 and now has two stores in Cambodia as well as stockists in Shanghai, Hong Kong, New York, Turin, Johannesburg and Madagascar. His customer is an adventurous woman who wants clothes that look as good as they feel on her skin. 'I make one-off pieces without a pattern and allow the fabrics to create the shapes through draping and hand-stitching the way Madeleine Vionnet did it in the 1920s and 1930s. For prêt-à-porter I use patterns and sizes. Both methods are interesting and give my clients exclusivity and choices.'

The designer hosts catwalk shows in Dakar and has taken part in Africa Fashion Week in Johannesburg. At the *ARISE* New York Fashion Week show for Spring/Summer 2010, his collection of artfully constructed dresses conjured up romance with sunset hues ebbing and flowing like rippled water across his pin tucked, crocheted and tie-dyed silks. 'I had a dream about dressing a young woman for her honeymoon in Madagascar. Her suitcase is full of magnificent, versatile pieces to seduce her prince with. Everything was soft and luxurious and played with the border between the manipulated fabrics and the 1970s silhouettes.'

For Autumn/Winter 2010/11 Raisina made a triumphant return to Paris. Cashmere minidresses and 'silk waffle' trouser suits were paired with footless socks, scarves and hoods made from velvet crocheted flowers. 'I looked to the 1930s jazz era to come up with a monochrome palette and mixed these with earthy shades, which represent my country. Just like Josephine Baker sang 'J'ai Deux Amours', I too have two loves – Madagascar and Paris.'

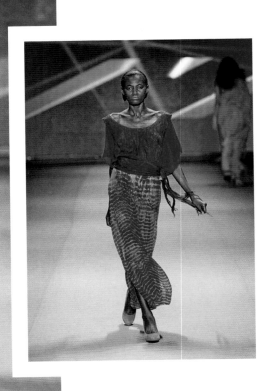

Raisina's delicate, handwoven textiles have found their way into collections by YSL, Christian Dior and Christian Lacroix.

OMER ASIM & MAYA ANTOUN

Great Minds

Omer Asim and Maya Antoun attended schools on opposite sides of the road in Khartoum, Sudan, as children but didn't meet until 2008 in London. Asim was instantly impressed by Antoun's fine silver jewellery. Likewise, Antoun was enamoured by Asim's minimal, serrated womenswear and so they decided to collaborate. 'We found that we shared similar backgrounds, design philosophies, and that our pieces synchronised', says Antoun. 'Our mediums are different, which enables us to bring a fresh perspective to each other's work.'

Asim studied architecture and psychology but an interest in visual anthropology led him to fashion. He has worked for Maurice Sedwell, Kristian Aadnevik and Vivienne Westwood and debuted his label at London Fashion Week for Spring/ Summer 2010 with a range of oblique garments cut from circle-like patterns. 'I find the concept of fashion and trends distasteful. My ultimate objective is to un-design cloth to create an aesthetic that borders between the pre- and post-modern', he says.

Antoun studied art and 3D design before specialising in jewellery at Central Saint Martins. She has developed ties with artisans in Khartoum and Kinshasa, DRC, to produce contemporary designs based on traditional styles and techniques and specialises in filigree, an ancient skill with a history that spans Europe, Asia and Africa. Her aim is to promote fair trade partnerships and challenge the parameters of dying crafts.

Joining forces for Spring/Summer 2011, Asim first thought about primitive clothing and Lucy's Baby, the earliest fossilised remains of man found in Ethiopia. Each piece was made from a single piece of uncut cloth not unlike the Sudanese *thoub*. 'It's a basic yet endlessly complex, elegant and progressive way of dressing when applied to prevailing expectations of functionality, which I achieved through sewing, zips and lightweight corsetry. The silhouettes were accidental and dishevelled.' Antoun's pendants, rings and cuffs were in part based on amulets and talismans and inspired by the now rare jewellery of the nomadic Beja and Bedouin tribes of northeastern Sudan. 'I like the idea of using existing vocabulary in order to make the traditional jewellery of the future, thereby creating a continuation in the history of African jewellery.'

Her pieces for Autumn/Winter 2011/12 continued along the same themes, becoming more streamlined and subtle, as a reflection of Asim's all-black collection of abstract, pure forms. 'Our creative relationship is constantly evolving and growing', she says. 'The longer we work together, the more our joint expression of human history becomes fine tuned.'

Bespoke
Couturier

OZWALD
BOATENG

Ozwald Boateng has broken boundaries in British menswear and earned international acclaim for his intuitive tailoring, innovative use of colour and daredevil attitude to doing business. Born in London to Ghanaian immigrants in 1967, he started making clothes aged 16, opened a studio in 1991 and in 1994 was the first tailor to have a show during Paris Fashion Week. At the age of 28, he became the youngest – and first black – tailor to move onto Savile Row, the bastion of gentlemen's tailoring. He won Best Menswear Designer at the British Fashion Awards in 2000 and was appointed creative director of Givenchy Homme in 2003. He had an exhibition devoted to him at the Victoria & Albert Museum, London, in 2005 and received an OBE in 2006. His flagship store, designed by British Ghanaian architect David Adjaye, was unveiled in 2007.

'I love what Savile Row represents and the significance of tailoring in British society, so being able to influence it has been important for me', he says of his trajectory. 'I've rooted everything in British tailoring but my heritage has also influenced my way of using colour, without a doubt. It's about taking something traditional and making it new. It's about understanding how to cut suits, develop fabrics and find new innovative techniques.'

His influence stretches home to Ghana, where in 2007 he hosted the African Union Power of Unity summit to celebrate the country's 50th anniversary of independence. The event was attended by 53 leaders and was aimed at rebranding Africa. 'The fashion show was saying to all of these presidents that Africa has the potential to be the greatest place on Earth. It controls over 50 per cent of the world's natural resources so the concept of poverty just doesn't make sense. Get the infrastructure right and there will be a boom in Africa like no continent has ever seen.'

The British-born tailor has become a Savile Row stalwart yet his understanding and use of colour belongs to Ghana.

In 2010 Boateng marked 25 years in fashion with his first show at London Fashion Week. Held at the Leicester Square Odeon, the blockbuster presentation featured sharp suits in acid hues, equestrian tailoring, leather hunting attire and sedate tuxedos from his Autumn/Winter 2010/11 and Spring/Summer 2011 collections. He cast 100 models, the largest number of men London Fashion Week has ever seen on one catwalk, in a diverse range of ages, creeds and colours. 'I didn't want to do a retrospective. Instead I conveyed my width of experience by showing 100 different ways to wear my clothes. The volume was a representation of time, and you really felt the presence of so many men.'

2011 sees the release of *A Man's Story*, a documentary film by director Varon Bonicos that was 12 years in the making. It marks the highs, such as his triumphs in Hollywood dressing the likes of Will Smith, Laurence Fishburne, Spike Lee and Jamie Foxx, as well as the lows, including a burglary and his divorce. 'The film has its own flow, truth and energy, which has nothing to do with me. The point it's making is that no one can tell you who you are – how to be a man – only you can work that out through experience.'

His own story is defined by the cut of a man's jib. 'It's a tailor's duty to create a suit that fits perfectly and brings out the wearer's best attributes. It's what I work for, because if someone feels good, he shares that with the rest of the world.'

'It's a tailor's duty to create a suit that fits perfectly and brings out the wearer's best attributes.'

From moodboard to catwalk: Boateng enlisted 100 male models to storm his London Fashion Week catwalk show in 2010 wearing a wide variety of looks, after which they marched in unison up to his flagship store on Savile Row, stopping traffic in their wake.

MATAANO

Sisters in Style

Twin sisters Ayaan and Idyl Mohallim keep things simple with their label Mataano. 'We want to create clothes that women can feel instantly feminine and attractive wearing', says Idyl. Born in Washington DC and raised in Mogadishu, their family returned to the US to avoid civil war in Somalia when the twins were aged nine. Their mother gave them fashion magazines as a way of helping them learn English and the girls were hooked. 'We loved to express ourselves through fashion and realised that we had to dress a certain way to better assimilate ourselves with our fellow American students. Fashion helped us fit in.'

Idyl went to university in Michigan, Ayaan in Boston, although neither studied fashion. It was only when they reconvened in New York that they began to realise their dream by interning at Betsey Johnson and Jill Stuart. Mataano ('twins' in Somali) started in Spring/Summer 2009 with a capsule collection of brightly coloured silk dresses and a month later they were invited onto *Oprah* for an episode about young moguls. Ensuing collections have grown in confidence, scope and size.

Spring/Summer 2010 took them on 'a spiritual journey to North Africa' to celebrate the females of the Ouled Nail Berber tribe in Algeria, who leave home at a young age to become dancers. They wear dresses layered with scarves and drape their wealth of silver and gold coins around their heads and bodies. The collection reinterprets this world-weary elegance through long taffeta skirts, shapeless dirac dresses, midriff-baring tops and oversized jewellery.

They showed their Spring/Summer 2011 collection, a nostalgic take on late 1950s styles using Italian shantung and printed organza, in Addis Ababa, New York and Johannesburg. And their Autumn/Winter 2011/12 collection of *Annie Hall*-style 1970s jersey and silk tea dresses, blouses and jumpsuits in sand, olive, nude, tangerine and mustard took centre stage at *ARISE* Magazine Fashion Week – Lagos 2011. 'We want to help redefine what African style means and share the diversity, depth and beauty that African fashion offers. It is the second largest continent in the world and can no longer be defined by a handful of clichéd fashion descriptions. In this age of globalisation our influences should be global and so too are our customers.'

'We want to help redefine what African style means and share the diversity, depth and beauty that African fashion offers.'

Lanre Da Silva Ajayi has had a life-long obsession with 1940s English fashion, from the 'make do and mend' wartime designs to the post-1945 resurgence of soft, feminine styles inspired by Christian Dior's New Look. Examining the archives of the period's royal couturiers such as Norman Hartnell, Hardy Amies and DAKS, the Nigerian designer's collections encompass restrained suiting and regal ballgowns. Yet each piece also exudes her distinctly African, eye-catching aesthetic. 'My fascination with the 1940s is simple. Women back then were particular about their looks and took care and time over themselves. They knew how to show off their curves in a ladylike, tasteful manner and dressed like they were queens', she says.

Ajayi started making clothes for herself and her friends while studying finance in the UK and established the label in Lagos in 2005. 'At first I found it hard to identify a customer because my designs were out of the ordinary and came as a bit of a shock to the average Nigerian woman. But today the local fashion industry and consumer are far more confident. My clothes cater to how bold and brilliant women want to dress themselves in today's ever-changing world.'

She's shown in Johannesburg, New York, Lagos and London and has done three ranges in association with Dutch wax print giants Vlisco. Each season is a deliberate reinvention from the previous one but none more so than Autumn/Winter 2011/12, which received a standing ovation at *ARISE* Magazine Fashion Week – Lagos 2011. Entitled The Modern Age, the show began with a series of demure waist-defining day dresses, camisoles, siren suits and safari shorts in lace, velvet and satin and graduated to long mermaid and maxi dresses in blossom-print French silk with petal sleeves. While the models' hair was pulled back into austere buns, there was a distinct lack of rationing when it came to trimmings. Gold sequins, beads, Swarovski crystals and leaf-like appliqué drowned the collection in a glittering sea of nostalgic romance.

Silver Siren

LANRE DA SILVA AJAYI

Black Coffee's thoroughly cerebral, meticulously constructed womenswear was born at a time when South Africa was facing a crossroads. Jacques van der Watt – who had grown up in a traditional Afrikaan family, studied both English and Japanese pattern-cutting techniques at Leggatts Design Academy (his graduate collection was all reversible) and worked as a costume designer – launched the label in 1998, shortly after the end of apartheid. 'It was inevitable that the country's search for a new African identity would be part of my own design process', he says. 'At the time designer fashion was considered only for occasion wear. Black Coffee was part of the new guard.'

Alongside other early pioneers such as David West, Abigail Betz and Stoned Cherrie, van der Watt forged a fresh frontier in South African fashion. His onus on the form and functionality of clothing over the frivolity of trends garnered an influential following. Joined by designer and stylist Danica Lepen in 2004, Black Coffee accumulated numerous accolades, including the 2009 Mercedes-Benz Award for Fashion, which took them to Berlin Fashion Week. They also introduced Everyone Can Be a Designer, a secondary range of mutable garments that leave the decision as to how they're worn up to the wearer, before Lepen's departure in 2010.

BLACK COFFEE

Bastion of
Bauhaus

Inspiration often stems from Africa. Safari wardrobes, Himba culture, Xhosa dress and local hairstyles have all proved starting points for collections, but the end results land far from their sources. For example, Autumn/Winter 2010/11's calm, confident range of cocoon and comforter coats referenced the proportions of African masks. Each one was oversized and imposing in scale yet softened by padding, quilting and faceting, as well as a dusky colour palette of putty, peach, smoke and mint. Reminiscent of Paul Poiret's designs from the 1910s, the outerwear, worn over the brand's signature concept dresses, made the models on the *ARISE* New York Fashion Week catwalk look like elegant aquatic mammals. 'I was particularly interested in how Picasso was influenced by African masks in his paintings and played with fragmented layers that build up volume and shape to create a Cubist effect. The looks might have seemed strange at first but they were actually very pretty.'

Spring/Summer 2011 was dominated by futuristic, boxy silhouettes covered in origami appliqué while Autumn/Winter 2011/12 saw van der Watt explore oversized, asymmetric shapes with pinching and pleating detailing. Three-tiered tulle dresses cascaded in shades of olive, royal purple and mud brown and jumpsuits were also given a multi-functional treatment. 'My work happens very organically, it is always a natural progression from one collection to the next. This season was a concise collection for the creative, adventurous woman.'

Picasso's 1907 painting *Les Demoiselles d'Avignon* inspired Black Coffee's Cubist coats for Autumn/Winter 2010/11.

Backstage at SA Fashion Week, where Black Coffee showed the Spring/Summer 2011 collection Form, Function and Furniture.

Renaissance
Woman

MOMO

With degrees in business, international communications, fashion marketing and styling to her name, Fati Asibelua launched Momo as a fabric shop in Abuja in 2000. She expanded into a fully fledged womenswear and footwear brand, opened a second store, and started a line of home and lifestyle products too. She's shown in Johannesburg, London, New York and Paris and has become a port of call in her native Nigeria among well-dressed, well-travelled, well-heeled women seeking unfussy fashion and original prints.

What first interested you in fashion?
From a young age I've been intrigued by the way that stylish people wear their clothes and what it says about them – I see fashion as a language that communicates a story about an individual. I began by working with fabrics and textile development remains an integral element of my design process. My passion is for opulent fabrics, African prints and timeless looks.

Where do you find inspiration?
African culture is always my starting point. I draw upon nature, the arts and the uplifting beats of African music. Africa has an immensely diverse heritage, combining sensitivity with simplicity and instinct with innovation.

Was your Autumn/Winter 2009/10 collection, which you showed both in New York and London, a pivotal moment for the brand?
Yes. The prints were inspired by the energies of safari wildlife. I reinvented animal prints using a pixilation effect in grey and bronze and kept the shapes minimal. In New York the models wore caps but in London I wanted the show to be more urban so I made geles using metallic fabrics and latex. Jourdan Dunn and Alek Wek looked amazing in them.

Fati Asibelua's 'passion for opulent fabrics, African prints and timeless looks' is well received in Abuja, London, New York and Paris.

Describe your recent collections.

For Autumn/Winter 2010/11, I created some very graphic, sharp pieces in jacquard, fur and brocade and by contrast the finishings were delicate with sheer organza linings and silk georgette bindings. My colour palette was predominantly black and navy with metallic threading and a splash of pink. For Spring/Summer 2011, I incorporated a collage of traditional prints including tie dye, reptile and wax prints in energising shades of yellow, red and orange against black and white silks, satins and lightweight knits. The shapes included sheath dresses, relaxed shorts and pencil skirts.

What are your hopes for the Nigerian fashion industry?

Nigeria has a wealth of talented, emerging designers and local craftsmen and the local scene is thriving. Now we must work together to put in place a proper infrastructure and promote ourselves to an international audience. Nigerian designers are ready to be recognised.

What drives you?

Every day brings new rewards and I believe tomorrow's rewards will be even greater. During the shows, to see the collection come to life after sleepless nights and hours of preparation is certainly one of the most rewarding aspects of my work.

Power
Couple

BUNMI
KOKO

'Strength.' 'Femininity.' 'Innovation.' 'Luxury.' These are all words that crop up time and time again in conversation with Bunmi Olaye, creative director of Bunmi Koko, a London-based brand with an ambitious vision.

Born and raised in Ibadan, Nigeria, and schooled in the UK, Olaye met her business and life partner Francis Udom while attending the University of East London and they launched Bunmi Koko (*bunmi* means 'God gave me' in Yoruba, *koko* means 'my other half' in Efik) in 2009. The debut Autumn/Winter 2010/11 collection, Geisha's Reform, examined the elaborate folding involved in traditional Japanese dressing and the folds of flowers to come up with tubular pleating techniques that appear on the shoulders of wrapover and waist-cinching dresses in hot-house hues.

Pleating, prints and catwalk theatrics express an aura of powerful femininity in each collection.

For Spring/Summer 2011's Matriarch collection, they paid their respects to Udom's ancestor Mary Slessor, a Scottish missionary known as the White Queen who lived with the Efiks in Calabar and helped outlaw cannibalism and the killing of twins at birth. The collection also investigates the Ekpe masquerade. A powerful cult in pre-colonial Nigeria, the Efik worshipped a mysterious forest-dwelling being, represented in ceremonial masquerade by a man in a monstrous multicoloured wool, hemp and raffia costume. Such a figure bounced menacingly down the catwalk at their shows, followed by a line of fierce, warrior-like looks. Exaggerated Victorian silhouettes in fiery shades of red, ochre, black and white were accessorised with bells, pom-poms and feathered masks.

'Matriarch was about celebrating female empowerment, domination and escapism. It was also a cultural fusion between Nigeria and Great Britain and made a statement about royalty and status', says Olaye. The collection earned Bunmi Koko the Emerging International Designer of the Year award at Africa Fashion Week 2010 and was also shown off-schedule at London Fashion Week.

For Autumn/Winter 2011/12 Kaleidoscopia reinterpreted scientific and philosophic discoveries of light, from stars to fibre optics, through prism-like 3D digital prints that played havoc with the electromagnetic spectrum. The shapes remained powerful, while velvet, patent leather, organza and silk jersey were festooned with phosphorescent Swarovski crystals, sequins and appliqué. Bunmi Koko debuted the brand in Nigeria at *ARISE* Magazine Fashion Week – Lagos 2011, and at New York Fashion Week for Spring/Summer 2012. But their proudest moment to date remains unparalleled. 'We met Nelson Mandela privately at his home in Johannesburg in 2010. I don't know what will ever top that!'

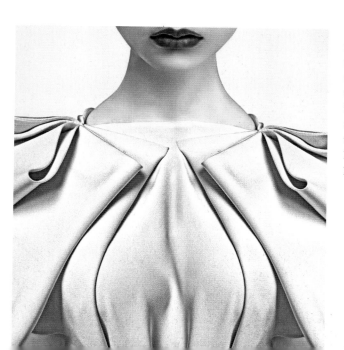

For Nkwo Onwuka's show at *ARISE* Magazine Fashion Week – Lagos 2011, she transformed her models into charmingly gawky tropical birds. Wearing feather crowns and neckpieces, and encased in bright orange, royal purple and lime-green fabrics, each one paused on the catwalk to stretch and flutter her imaginary wings. A Masai blanket-inspired wave print added to the collection's sense of movement, while quilted pockets and roomy jumpsuits accentuated hips.

For Onwuka, fashion has always been a flight of fantasy. Growing up between Oxford, UK, and Nsukka, Nigeria, she spent her childhood 'making puppets, rag dolls and costumes' under the watchful eye of her seamstress mother. 'It never ceased to amaze me how she would be working on a piece of fabric before I went to bed and then, as if by magic, it would be transformed into the most beautiful dress by the time I woke up', she recalls.

She studied psychology, interned at a number of fashion houses in New York and London, and debuted Nkwo at Kulture2Couture 2007, a show for emerging black designers held at the Victoria & Albert Museum, London. The collection, titled Feathers from an Angel, centred on floaty silk dresses festooned with feathers, and won the event's Phoenix award. 'The collection embraced the freedom and innovation of the 1960s and 1970s and the *joie de vivre* of African style. It's what I call Afro bohemian chic.'

Bird of
Paradise
NKWO

Nkwo's feathery, wraparound designs embrace 'the freedom and innovation of the 1960s and 1970s and the *joie de vivre* of African style'.

She's since shown in Berlin, New York, Johannesburg, Nairobi and Kingston, and the brand has become synonymous with her inventive use of batik braiding and the retro wrap, a reinterpretation of the African wrapper. Onwuka has also introduced the diffusion line Afromania by Nkwo, and her aim is to make Nkwo 100% environmentally and socially responsible.

Perhaps her most profound statement to date was her Keepers of the Faith dress, which she made for charity in 2010. It explored the rise in churches where Christianity and local beliefs have combined to produce a deep-rooted fear in God and supernatural entities and where women now play strong roles as pastors and prophets. 'The dress symbolises the lightness of angels and the dark mysticism and rituals of indigenous practices, which are locked in a cycle of protection from one against harm from the other.'

In West African adinkra textiles, the sankofa bird symbol represents learning from the past and feathers themselves are used as brushes to apply adire patterns onto fabric with cassava paste. With her use of African fabrics and feathers, Onwuka's work becomes a wearable expression of female empowerment and freedom.

(Un)traditionalist

STIAAN LOUW

Stiaan Louw is one of the most progressive voices in South African fashion. Awarded Best Menswear Designer at the Africa Fashion Awards 2010 and appearing on a cover of *Wallpaper** magazine, the buzz around him is both palpable and well-deserved. Louw's androgynous, multi-layered collections explore male sexuality and the clashes between social tribes, issues that intrigue him as an Afrikaan working in a fledgling democracy and equally fledgling men's fashion market.

The Durbanville-born designer fell for fashion during the grunge-obsessed early 1990s, his first crush being Ann Demeulemeester. He studied at the Haute Couture School of Fashion Design in Cape Town, where he developed an affinity for cut, construction and hand-tailoring, and on graduating in 2000 he worked as a stylist and accessories designer. He ran a womenswear brand between 2004 and 2007 but struggled to find a visual language and in 2008 he made a natural progression to menswear. 'I made wearable pieces with subtle depth using different textures and fabrics, all in tones of black. I felt liberated and the positive response was instant and surprising', he says.

His sixth menswear collection for Autumn/Winter 2011/12, aptly titled 6, moved Louw's tribe themes beyond his initial obsessions with youth culture into posing questions about what it means to be African and whether there is an unifying African aesthetic. Studying the traditions of wrapping and draping in Masai, Middle Eastern, Greco-Roman and Indian cultures, he released the collection through a series of photographs featuring an often nude male model immersed in water.

For the collection's catwalk debut at Joburg Fashion Week, models were given white painted faces and clay mud-covered hands and feet and resembled windswept, regal nomads in billowing overcoats, loose-belted caftans, oversized vests, heavy necklaces and harem pants. 'My campaign images and catwalk presentations are often challenging. As a white designer working in Africa I've often felt a sense of displacement but this collection presents Africa as the cradle of mankind. We are all African, irregardless of ethnicity, cultural background or sexuality.'

Louw's controversial approach has worked. His menswear has been embraced by a wide group of clients and he's now relaunching a capsule womenswear collection, too. 'I'm positive about the future of South Africa. Fashion, as with the other arts, has the power to inspire and transcend boundaries. Success lies in global integration and positioning Africa as a fertile source of design talent.'

Louw's androgynous
collections delve deeply
into male sexuality and
South Africa's social tribes.

'As a white designer working in Africa I've often felt a sense of displacement but this collection presents Africa as the cradle of mankind.'

LOIN CLOTH & ASHES

Daydreamer

Anisa Mpungwe is a dreamer. Born in the Tanzanian capital, Dar es Salaam, she spent her early years living in a beach house and fantasising about *Alice's Adventures in Wonderland* and Salvador Dalí. 'The sea and sand was my front yard. My father was an ambassador. He wore the most unparalleled suits and came home from business trips with amazing toys and clothes for me. My life was really magical, inside and out. I guess that's how I started drawing fabulous dresses and characters with egg-shaped heads', she says.

Her family moved to South Africa in 1994, where she studied fashion at the Midrand Graduate Institute. She took a postgraduate course at the London College of Fashion in 2007, and returned to Johannesburg to intern with African Mosaique and Black Coffee. Within a year she had established Loin Cloth & Ashes. Her debut collection of pleated and gathered tops and dresses won the South African *Elle* New Talent Award and took her to Stockholm Fashion Week.

Her two ensuing collections, which gave stylistic nods to such disparate references as pop art, Lily Allen, *The Transformers* and Tim Burton, prepared her to show at the *ARISE* New York Fashion Week show for Spring/Summer 2010. Her collection concentrated on structured shapes that accentuated curves. Models swayed from one side of the catwalk to the other in billowing harem pants, origami motif-printed tops, suede tailored jackets, short tweed skirts, jodhpurs and felt minidresses featuring leaf-like folding. Shades of grey and black were punctuated with cobalt-blue Perspex jewellery.

She dedicated the collection to Ifakara, her father's home village. 'It's an old, forgotten place with an innate splendour. The landscape, the old buildings, the children running in the dirt roads with no shoes on, and the peace of the place reminded me of what was important in life. The collection was me going back to basics.'

Tanzania's Mpungwe
crosses arts and crafts with
sophisticated draping and
tailoring.

Far from home, however, Mpungwe found the overall experience of being part of New York Fashion Week overwhelming. 'I lived my dream without really, mentally being there. I feel like it was someone else that did all that work and all those media interviews and drank all that coffee. I even started crying during one TV interview, I just couldn't believe I was showing in the same tent as all those other big designers I grew up idolising.'

She's shown her most recent collections in Angola and Johannesburg and cemented her flair for ultra-ladylike tailoring and draping and daring use of florals, African prints and costume jewellery. Autumn/Winter 2011/12 paired sunglasses with snoods, turbans with knitwear and pencil skirts with unusually placed bustles. 'I make clothes for women who follow their hearts' desires and dare to be different', Mpungwe says. She's referring to her customer but could equally be talking about herself.

The Ifakara collection
conjures up the innate
splendour of a forgotten,
peaceful landscape.

Tsemaye Binitie grew up on a diet of Versace, Moschino and Missoni in 1980s Lagos and London, sowing the seeds of his own designs, which now revolve around 'unabashed glamour' and 'the perfect cut'. He graduated from Kingston University in 2004 and got a feel for the industry through working for John Richmond, Burberry and Stella McCartney. His first solo 'project' in 2009 was called Blackout and comprised 10 little black dresses, which he dedicated to significant black women in his life.

In contrast, his Spring/Summer 2010 collection, In Livin Color, looked to his young nieces' rainbow outfits and toys to come up with a range of variegated violet, canary yellow, white and red bondage dresses and daytime separates in washed silk crepe and chiffon. The line has grown to include swimwear and a T-shirt range but he always brings it back to body-conscious, downtown dresses. For Autumn/ Winter 2011/12 his mother Sade was his starting point, or more precisely a nostalgic memory he has of her from the early 1980s. 'She was going on a trip to Paris and packing pieces that made her feel distinctly Nigerian but allowed her to blend into European society. I focused on my Nigerian heritage, colours and prints.'

He found a vintage animal-print scarf in Portobello Market and manipulated the pattern to create a jungle-striped silk blazer, pleated trousers and a turban. Italian wool, cashmere, silk, guipure lace and leather brought panelled dresses, trapeze tops and leggings to life in black, tropical orange, slate and flesh tones. The collection was well received at *ARISE* Fashion Week – Lagos 2011, where he was selected to participate in the *ARISE* show at New York Fashion Week the following season. With this exposure, Binitie will be one step closer to his ultimate goal: 'I want my brand to be in every woman's wardrobe!'

TSEMAYE BINITIE

Glamazon

Binitie's time at Burberry and Stella McCartney is evident in his take on global glamour.

TIFFANY AMBER

Cruise
Controller

After church, Sundays in Lagos are about one thing – jumping on a yacht and cruising out to sea. And to be dressed right for the occasion, there's only one woman to call – Folake Folarin-Coker. Her label Tiffany Amber offers resortwear and soft, floaty dresses for ladies who lunch, work and sail.

She was born in Lagos, schooled in Switzerland, England and Scotland and relocated to Abuja in 1998 to become a lawyer. But when she realised the career 'was nothing like *LA Law*' she channelled her energies into making clothes for herself and her friends instead. 'I put on a fashion show and it was so successful I haven't looked back since', she says. 'Back then there were no indigenous ready-to-wear designers so I was filling a huge gap in the market.'

Her first collection comprised linen tunics and chiffon caftans (she sold 365 pieces in five days) and today she has four stand-alone stores. 'Fashion isn't theatre: my clothes don't overpower the wearer, but rather enhance her style.' Tiffany Amber won Designer of the Year at Africa Fashion Week 2009, Johannesburg, and has also shown in New York, Nairobi, Paris and Luanda.

Her Spring/Summer 2011 collection, Raw Glamour, transported Studio 54 from New York to St Tropez with a range of silky boyfriend jackets, wide-legged trousers, city shorts and butterfly jumpsuits in aqua, spring green, daffodil and iris. And for Autumn/Winter 2011/12's Fearless Luxury collection, her 1970s disco queens came bedecked in crushed velvet suits, long and lacy cowl-neck gowns and double-breasted blazers. Key to the collection were four prints based on photographs by Victor Politis of beads, a product with a history steeped in trading, slavery and wealth in West Africa. Coral, crystal, amber, aqua, gold and viridian glass beads appear to drip down draped dresses, shirts and culottes. The collection won her Fashion Brand of the Year at the *ARISE* Magazine Fashion Week – Lagos 2011 and puts her well on her way to achieving her vision of becoming 'the premier African lifestyle brand'.

TEL: 339-1113

JAY
EMBROIDERIES

Tiffany Amber has grown from a range of tunics in 1998 to become one of Nigeria's biggest fashion brands.

'Fashion isn't theatre: my clothes don't overpower the wearer but rather enhance her style.'

BUKI AKIB

Quintessential
Nigerian

Buki Agbabiaka was born in Lagos in 1978 and grew up a few minutes' drive away from Fela Anikulapo-Kuti's Kalakuta Republic and Shrine nightclub. The throbbing birthplace of Afrobeat, which became the soundtrack to Nigerian dissidence, rebellion and uninhibited good times, was where Kuti reigned until his death in 1997. His reputation as an activist, showman, megalomaniac, outlaw and musical pioneer continues to resonate today. His sons Femi and Seun keep his music and his club alive, Broadway pays homage to him with the musical *FELA!*, a Hollywood biopic is planned and Agbabiaka has also given due reverence to him with her debut menswear collection.

Originally an actor, she went to London's Central Saint Martins to study illustration but ended up specialising in knitwear following a fruitful internship at British knitwear house Weardowney. After visiting a weaving factory in Nigeria, she could think of no better subject for her final collection than Kuti. 'Growing up in Lagos was an education in fashion in itself – I remember my parents' lavish parties attended by groomed men showing off gleaming, gold cufflinks as they smoked the finest cigars, and women who looked like models from *Ebony* magazine', she recalls. 'Fela was hailed as quintessentially Nigerian. He was a sex god and commanded attention with such ease and grace. I was worried at first about using such an iconic figure as my muse but fear always motivates me. Fela's music has taught me it's okay to be ruthless and take risks. So I did.'

Fela Kuti is the muse for this 'virile' collection, aimed at modern men willing to walk on the wild side.

Experimenting with radiant colours and textures, she mixed up deep purple, gold, fuchsia, grass-green and dusty bronze to recreate the 'heat and sweat of the Shrine experience', and combined silk, Lurex, viscose and cotton yarns to make three-dimensional patterns, which she put together with vintage patchwork ase-oke and tassel adornments. Looks included drop-crotch tracksuit trousers, romper suits, mesh shirts, string vests and giant coats.

'He had a distinctive style and manner, which I tried to capture in the extravagant swimming trunks – an allusion to Fela's favourite Speedos – and the virile high-waisted trousers with knitted patches. The heavy multicoloured jacket sums up Fela's ego. I wanted to make a bold statement about a modern-day Fela that brave guys from Lagos, Tokyo or London would wear. I'm sure Fela would have loved it too.'

The Fela collection was selected for the Central Saint Martins prestigious L'Oréal press show in 2010, and was also well received at *ARISE* Magazine Fashion Week – Lagos 2011. Agbabiaka is currently working on a line of Fela bags, and is building the brand to include womenswear and interior design. 'I am an artist first and foremost. I use design as a medium of expression and want the label to act as a storyteller. Africans should tell stories of Africa – past, present and future.'

Lagos meets Manhattan in the work of Bridget Awosika. Satisfying the demands of both the red-carpet socialite and the career-minded girl about town, Awosika is motivated by the 'energy and drive' of the women she has lived among in both cities and hopes that her designs make the wearer feel 'chic, sexy and confident'.

Awosika grew up between the USA and Nigeria and studied business at Howard University in Washington DC and fashion at Parsons The New School for Design, New York. She graduated in 2006, worked for Donna Karan and Giorgio Armani and returned home to Lagos in 2009, where her eveningwear quickly built up a clientele. She officially launched for Spring/Summer 2011 with a focus on neon shades, architectural lines and Nigerian fabrics, including tie-dye and ase-oke. Describing the collection as a 'youthful take on upscale', shapes ranged from sporty racerback dresses and boyish suiting to gala gowns, with asymmetry, accordion pleats, draping and fringing ensuring that the details provided drama. It went down well with her local fans.

For Autumn/Winter 2011/12, however, she was in a New York state of mind. 'I was thinking about city nights and how everyone there wears black as if it's a uniform. The collection was about movement, sophistication and androgyny. I drew on the texture and structure of the previous collection but this time the look was softened and more relaxed.' She shook up the almost all-black range with flashes of aubergine and cream across a range of SoHo (sheer buttoned-up shirts and stirrup trousers) and Upper East Side (long beaded and organza dresses) looks. 'It's my vision of what a progressive African woman wants to wear, wherever she may be. Africa has a voice in fashion at last. It's up to us as designers what we do with it.'

City Slicker

BRIDGET AWOSIKA

'Africa has a voice in
fashion at last. It's up to
us as designers what we
do with it.'

Many contemporary accessory designers look at the complex messages and meanings behind the different types of jewellery and adornments originating from tribes around the continent for inspiration, and continue to use readily available raw materials such as wood, shells, leather, feathers and semi-precious stones. The Zulus of southern Africa wore colour-coded beaded necklaces that acted as love letters. The Fulani women in Mali don a crown of amber to denote that they are married. Tuareg jewellery is silver and simple as a reflection of their austere nomadic lifestyles; their khomissar pendant is believed to ward off the evil eye. The Masai wear cowrie shells as a symbol of fertility. Bronze collars were bestowed on Bamum dignitaries in Cameroon in recognition of bravery. And gold is fashioned into royal and funereal jewellery by the Ashanti people of Ghana.

By combining these myriad influences with the latest fashion trends, technologies, methods and materials – not to mention re-appropriating tribal catwalk jewellery that has been offered up by the likes of Louis Vuitton and Diane von Furstenberg – designers reflect upon Africa's social flux and in doing so create a new layer in the annals of African adornment.

ACCESSORIES

Alex Folzi

Benin-born twins Fela and Fola Fagbure have always lived for fashion. 'To us it's art, it's life. We're drawn to anything attractive and impeccable', says Fola. They both moved from Nigeria to Canada to attend university and introduced Alex Folzi in 2010 while in their freshman year. The brand is now synonymous with vintage-inspired suitcases and trunks in a range of preppy colours. Each piece bears the Alex Folzi insignia, is finished with reinforced corners, nametags and sturdy straps and looks as though it should be stacked up on a luggage trolley at the Ritz.

Kwame Brako

Kwame Brako's strict Catholic upbringing in Ghana inspired his 2009 graduate collection at New York's Parsons The New School for Design. Head-to-toe looks explored the restrictions of a nun's habit but it was the shoes, Brako's abstract adaptation of 'cathedral architecture and stained-glass windows', that garnered the most attention. His steel-heeled platform boots won the inaugural Cesare Paciotti competition, which gave him the opportunity to have his designs hand-made in Italy. 'High heels are a discreet form of self-expression that women can enjoy. To me they represent sexual power and superiority', he says. 'I'm also drawn to the level of precision and confidence that African women put into their choice of ancestral outfits, ornate jewellery and elaborate headdresses.' His first commercial collection for 2011 assays the plumage and anatomy of migrant birds.

Anita Quansah

Statement necklaces assembled from a treasure trove of chains, pearls, beads, shells and recycled textiles have become Anita Quansah's calling card. The Chelsea College of Art & Design graduate was born in London to Nigerian and Ghanaian parents and worked for everyone from ASOS to Christian Lacroix before establishing her label in 2006. She's since designed catwalk pieces for Jewel by Lisa, Nkwo and Eki Orleans and been championed by pop stars Estelle, Shingai Shoniwa and Keisha Buchanan. 'My grandmother was a well-known seamstress in Onitsha [Nigeria] and I remember one day discovering her store of shimmering embroideries. It was like heaven opening up. I've had an emotional connection to textiles ever since', she says. 'My passion now is for transforming found materials into colourful, original and ethical pieces.'

Albertus Swanepoel

Award-winning milliner Albertus Swanepoel is the go-to guy
for catwalk designers at New York Fashion Week. In recent
seasons he has made vinyl beanies for Alexander Wang,
elaborate tiaras for Erin Fetherston, sun hats for Suno, pom-
pom helmets for Proenza Schouler and feather-trimmed
fedoras for Carolina Herrera, the style he's now best known
for. Born in Pretoria, he was a celebrated womenswear designer
in South Africa by the time he relocated to New York in 1987.
He trained in millinery under Janine Galimard, Lola and Lynne
Mackey and sold his first hats to Paul Smith in 1993. By 2003 he
had gone it alone and in 2009 his work was selected by Stephen
Jones for his exhibition Hats – An Anthology at the Victoria &
Albert Museum, London. 'Hats give a person instant character,
which is so important in our globalised world', he says. 'I'm
influenced by the cultural diversity of South Africa and use
traditional textiles such as shwe shwe. The longer I am away
from Africa, the more I seem to use it in my work.'

Free Peoples Rebellion

'My brand name pays homage to the history of Liberia, which was founded by freed slaves from America. It's also a reminder of the country's two civil wars', says Sarah Williams of Free Peoples Rebellion. The first war in 1989 prevented her parents from returning home from New York, where she was born. Yet they ensured that their daughter embraced her heritage and knew 'the pleasures of palm butter rice, fufu, and pepper soup'. She worked in community health but retrained at the Fashion Institute of Technology in 2009 after accessories she made from Liberian lapas fabric proved popular. Her design process begins by choosing a strong female musician as her muse (songs by Ebony Bones and Santigold have christened two collections). She then names each piece after an African tribe whose adornments inspire her own – her Mursi earrings refer to the Ethiopian ethnic group whose women wear clay plates in their lower lips. 'My icons are indigenous women who transform themselves into works of art using their surrounding resources', she says. Part of the profits go to youth organisations in Liberia.

For his Autumn/Winter 2011/12 show, which provided the finale for Joburg Fashion Week, David Tlale closed down Nelson Mandela Bridge to traffic to create a 284-metre-long catwalk. The only vehicle allowed was a Harley-Davidson motorbike upon which the designer was perched to make his entrance. The collection consisted of an epic 92 looks worn by as many models and local celebrities and included sumptuous printed womenswear and menswear, plus-size styles, his first bag range, a collaborative jewellery line and bridalwear, which all came together under the theme of Made in the City. He dedicated the show to 'Madiba' and topped the spectacle off with a fireworks display. It was an ambitious presentation and an example of exactly why he has become South African fashion's darling. 'The David Tlale brand is all about glamour and power', he says. 'It's daring, dramatic and defies convention.'

DAVID TLALE Hot Ticket

Tlale launched in 2003 and has since accumulated praise and status for his designs, which express a deep understanding of fabric, colour and texture while remaining as bold and theatrical as the designer himself. Often photographed on the gold throne that resides in his Johannesburg studio, he has chosen a cross as his brand logo and dresses every inch the rock star in leather and shades. His accolades range from being voted Best New Designer of the Year 2003 by the *SA Sunday Times* to being awarded Designer of the Year at Africa Fashion Week in 2009, and he's taken the brand to Swahili Fashion Week, Fashion Business Angola, Paris Fashion Week and Cape Town Fashion Week.

Wherever he shows, there remains an essence of Africa in his work. His Spring/Summer 2010 collection, shown at the *ARISE* show at New York Fashion Week, is a case in point. 'The theme of the collection was cultural intimacy. I used ostrich egg shell beads from the South African San tribe, horns and fabrics from Swaziland and my signature tailoring to create high-end ready-to-wear pieces.' Women's plaited boleros with pointed shoulders, dramatically draped dresses and silk trousers with fringing from waist to ankle were a modern take on occasion wear while men's gold and pink silk suits were worn with paisley shirts and Elizabeth ruffs.

'The David Tlale brand is all about glamour and power. It's daring, dramatic and defies convention.'

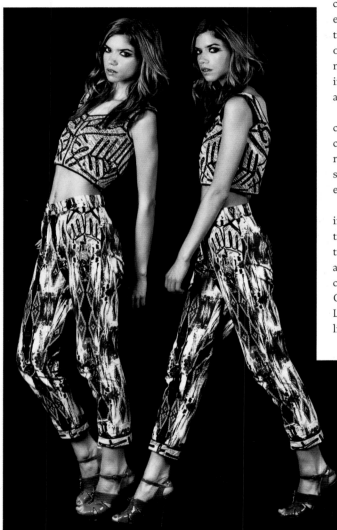

Orie Omatsola spent her youth in Lagos picking out fabrics with her mother Lola at the local markets. Twenty-one years later, nothing much has changed. Of her four collections to date, two are dedicated to Lola, and no design gets passed without her approval. 'My mum has taught me about the power of simplicity and our collaborative approach is magic almost every time', Omatsola says.

Omatsola took a summer course in fashion at Milan's NABA School of Design in 2007 and began the label in 2009 while completing a BA in art history at the University of Manchester. Ré Bahia's focus is on easy shapes that allow the fabrics and colours to take precedence. Important to the brand is an embroidery technique called kohbaslot, originally devised by the Creole people of Sierra Leone and customarily worn by older generations. Omatsola learnt the technique from her mother and has renamed the method *uma* (meaning 'secret' in her father's Itsekiri language). In her hands it gives Ankara an intricate, touchy feely finish.

The craft came alive in her Autumn/Winter 2011/12 collection where it added an authentic spirit to a range of body-conscious minidresses, crop tops and shorts. Exposed zips lent a raw edge while other pieces in the collection, such as a sea-hued silk caftan and a Halston-inspired white pleated maxi dress, expressed different sides of the Ré Bahia woman.

'She's someone who appreciates the workmanship that goes into each piece that ensures that no two garments are exactly the same', says Omatsola. 'For this collection I was listening to Adele's "Rolling in the Deep", so I was also thinking about a heartbroken woman. Those emotions come through in my choice of earthy colours.' The line is produced in Nigeria, where Omatsola also showed at *ARISE* Magazine Fashion Week – Lagos 2011. Naturally, her family filled the front row: 'I felt like the luckiest girl in the world.'

Mummy's Girl

RÉ BAHIA

'The workmanship that goes
into each piece ensures that
no two garments are exactly
the same.'

Lisa Folawiyo has been largely responsible for reinventing Ankara as a luxury fabric. She trained as a barrister but after the birth of her daughter in 2005, she had time to reflect on the African influences she saw on international catwalks and came up with the idea of embellishing the African-print cloth with sequins, beads and crystals. It took her three weeks to make one heavily encrusted skirt, which caused such ripples in Lagos fashion circles that Jewel by Lisa took off. 'Everyone just had to have one', says Folawiyo. 'I love patterns, textures and the juxtaposition of colours and wanted to turn Ankara into something special. People were intrigued.'

Early collections established her staples – the blazer, the shift dress, the maxi skirt – and an eye for bright prints and hand-finishing. She's since showed at Africa Fashion Week in Johannesburg and as part of *ARISE* shows at New York Fashion Week for Spring/Summer 2010 and Paris Fashion Week for Autumn/Winter 2010/11. These collections brought other materials, including leather, knitwear and silk, into the mix. 'Ankara is versatile and can transcend seasons and continents. My clothes speak of good design, cut and fabric and have a global point of view. Women from Bali to Milan can wear my brand while appreciating the fact that it is created and produced in Nigeria.'

Jewel by Lisa truly came into its own in Spring/Summer 2011 when Folawiyo introduced her own custom-made Ankara-inspired prints on cotton, georgette and royal and shantung silks. Entitled Global Minimalism, her Afro-geometric take on 'tribal' prints was a collaboration with textile designer Banke Kuku, whose credits include Burberry, Duro Olowu and Jasmine Di Milo. The digitally created patterns in shades of flint, berry, citron and honeycomb mixed seamlessly with Ankara while shapes remained refreshingly straightforward – trench dresses, pleated minis, cocoon shirts and cropped trousers.

JEWEL BY LISA

Star Bright

For Autumn/Winter 2011/12, shown at *ARISE* Magazine Fashion Week – Lagos 2011, Jewel by Lisa presented tapestry, batik, crocodile and African mud cloth-inspired prints on velvet, linen, silk, satin and chiffon in shades of lilac, pink, ivy and tobacco. Drop-waisted dresses with multiple hems, jumpsuits, bow blouses, waistcoats and leggings also showed a new maturity in garment construction. Catwalk accessories were a collaboration with Anita Quansah. 'This collection presented an ultra-modern sense of style and youthfulness that only comes with the wearer's inherent fashion know-how', she says. 'Above all, I'm saluting the fashion aplomb of the Nigerian woman who, when draped in her native attire, be it Ankara, lace or aso oke, epitomises African style.'

Ankara forms both the basis and the inspiration for Lisa Folawiyo's print-driven brand.

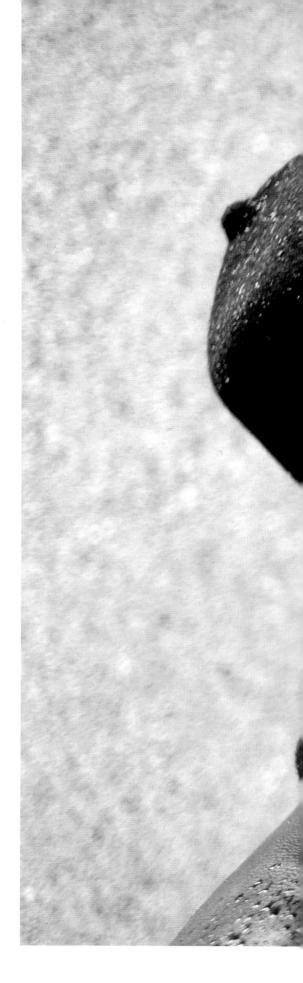

EMEKA ALAMS

Slave to the Rhythm

'The Western media only covers Africa on two occasions – if there is a corrupt election or a mass genocide. All those dazzling and progressive things I've witnessed in Africa – the art movements, expanding infrastructures, the peace that flourishes in the vast majority of the continent – don't get reported. This is where my objective for Gold Coast Trading Co. started. I strive to show the balanced reality of a modern Africa.'

This mission statement from US-born Nigerian Emeka Alams, founder of streetwear brand Gold Coast Trading Co., stems from his time living in Côte d'Ivoire and Ghana. During his college drop-out pilgrimage to West Africa he found himself in the crossfire of civil war in Abidjan in 2004. 'The whole thing was surreal, I was trapped in a house for two weeks with no food, phone or internet and with gunfire all around.' He was eventually evacuated but the incident, far from putting him off his homeland, convinced him to use his creativity to promote positive messages about it.

'In America you autopilot through life and then one day you drop dead. In Africa you feel every day, you experience how real life actually is. The colours and sounds mixed with the sun and the heat makes it a very singular experience. The people are warm and genuine, the culture is rich and powerful. There is nothing like knowing where you're from – seeing it with your own eyes, smelling it and tasting it. The things I saw changed my priorities.'

Following a stint as part of the urban collective 21MC, he began Gold Coast Trading Co. in 2008. Named after the historical term for the part of West Africa that became ground zero for the transatlantic slave trade in the 15th century, the name is Alams's rallying call to reclaim the region's ownership of its own resources. The first full collection for Spring/Summer 2010, Togo Waves and Road Maps, smothered T-shirts, knitwear, shorts and bags in seemingly ancient symbols and scriptures. The subsequent collection Youth of 1976 looked further south to pay respect to the Soweto Uprising, a series of student-led street demonstrations that protested the introduction of Afrikaans as the main language in South African schools, which saw several hundred slain by armed police. The range finds its modern male muses in Johannesburg's scene-making musicians Mpumi Mcata from BLK JKS and Spoek Mathambo.

Glibly describing the look of the line as 'something a Liberian warlord would wear', his actual client list includes UK/Nigerian musicians Afrikan Boy and Kele Okereke and he's also created graphics for Damian Marley, Nas and M.I.A. Currently based in New York, Alams wants eventually to relocate permanently to West Africa and take the production of the line with him. 'Fashion can't change the world, but what we choose to do with the opportunities it affords us can affect Africa in a nuturing way.'

Gold Coast Trading Co. revisits Africa's heart of darkness to take ownership of its culturally rich future.

Suzaan Heyns was born in Johannesburg and received a bursary from South African *Elle* to attend the city's London International School of Fashion. She's worked as a stylist and illustrator and ran the T-shirt brand Abraham Louisa with fellow stylist Louw Kotze. Her debut solo show at Cape Town Fashion Week 2009, featuring supermodel Jourdan Dunn, set the precedent for her theatrical, often macabre presentation style. Involving music, voiceovers, visuals and sets (in collaboration with art director Willem Kitshoff), the melodramatic mood created is always a reflection of her equally avant-garde, unrelenting designs.

Her Autumn/Winter 2011/12 show Die Vorm (That Form) at Joburg Fashion Week was no exception. A short film depicted men wearing surgical masks operating on a woman and using archaic instruments to open her up. But instead of blood, fabric spills out and forms an outfit that brings Heyns's female Frankenstein to life. 'The range looked at the mechanics of the body by raising the physicality of it to the surface, which in turn represents the unveiling of our hidden psyche', explains Heyns. Victorian-inspired tailoring for both men and women in leather, wool and jersey was torn, tightened, padded and pleated to suggest muscles, sinews and the inner organs. Ribbons and harnesses formed bones across corsetry in flesh tones, greys and blacks.

'I view fashion as sculpture with fabric, it's a form of architecture for a movable form. Inspiration is always fluid. It might be an abstract concept, something more concrete like origami [Spring/Summer 2009] or my Afrikaan heritage [Spring/Summer 2011]. It changes with each season but my aesthetic always remains hard and androgynous.'

She's collaborated with AngloGold Ashanti Auditions, Ivka Cica and Jeana Theron, and her boutique in Melville, one of Johannesburg's most creative hubs, further reveals the world according to Heyns: a story best told with the lights dimmed.

Fashion's
Frankenstein

SUZAAN HEYNS

Deola Sagoe is the grande dame of contemporary Nigerian fashion. Born in the 1960s, she studied business in Miami and finance in Lagos, but turned her back on the corporate world to work in her mother's tailoring studio as an embroidery designer for men's traditional wear. She established her brand in the late 1980s on the principle of pushing African handwoven fabrics into uncharted territories.

Since then she's shown everywhere from Cape Town to Rome and accrued numerous accolades for her earthy, feminine designs, among them being the MNet/AngloGold African Designs 2000 winner (for which she was nominated by US *Vogue*'s André Leon Talley). 'My lack of formal fashion education has made experience my teacher, but my innate ability has also heightened my fashion sense, and caused me to be a stickler for research and self-development', she says. 'Over the years my designs, construction and finishing have become increasingly sophisticated.'

Her most recent collections are indeed her best. For Autumn/Winter 2010/11 she looked at East African tribes and the military uniforms of 18th- and 19th-century Europe. Shown at the *ARISE* New York Fashion Week show, she transformed models Sessilee Lopez, Kinée Diouf, Oluchi Onweagba and Shena Moulton into modern-day Boudiccas in ase-oke body-conscious dresses, fishtail skirts, slim-fit trousers, combat coats and baby-doll dresses caged inside shredded Lycra. 'I've had a thing for military clothing since watching *An Officer and a Gentleman*. But I also wanted to bring out the strength of the African woman, who is now more liberated and independent but still retains her mystery and femininity.'

Queen Bee

DEOLA SAGOE

Spring/Summer 2011 was dedicated to 1950s pin-ups – think flirty hemlines, silver-screen monochromes and sweetheart necklines. And for Autumn/Winter 2011/12 she was transported to Japan. Velvet blanket coats, tie-dye culottes, kimono-style tops and lampshade skirts in lace, silk and crinkled ase-oke were full of Eastern promise. 'Nigerian style is unique. We are among the most glamorous and happy peoples in the world and our fashion reflects that', she says. 'As designers we face constraints in resources and infrastructure but this only makes us more innovative and detail-conscious. Fashion from the continent complements global influences but it should never lose its identity.'

'I want to bring out the strength of the African woman, who is now more liberated and independent but still retains her mystery and femininity.'

Costumier

A. SAUVAGE

Tailor, designer, stylist, photographer, filmmaker – the world of Adrien Sauvage encompasses many avenues but they all revolve around the modern gentleman's wardrobe. The Londoner with parents of Ghanaian and Ivorian descent has put his globe-trotting experiences from previous occupations as a professional basketball player and image consultant into the A. Sauvage ethos. 'I call it the art of dressing easy. I've gone through so many fashion foibles in my life that I now know what works. My suits are for guys who don't usually wear suits by making it simple to put a look together. It's all about mix and match tailoring', he says.

Each jacket in his 2010 collection catered to the time of day and pursuit – the country blazer, sports jacket, city boy suit – while trousers and ties came in complementary styles and colours. Design touches such as scallop collars on shirts, rope shoulders on jackets and side adjusters on trousers, paired with a palette of electric blue, plum, burnished orange and forest green, ensured that the end looks were daring yet understated.

Sauvage's surrealist short film *This Is Not a Suit* introduced the brand at London Fashion Week and was selected for the Sundance Film Festival. He also shot a series of photographs of people wearing his pieces who fell into one of two categories – Captains or Natives. 'It was a study in individualism. I went to Venice Beach to meet natives, unsung heroes who are celebrities in their own right. It's a place where skateboarders, basketball players and surfers all entwined in one diverse community. I got my collection out of a suitcase and asked them to put on what they felt reflected them.'

He returned to London to shoot his captains of industry (recognisable people whose work he admired), who included Bill Nighy, Mark Ronson, Coco Sumner, Plan B and Terry Gilliam. He then presented the captains and natives side by side on a blog with everyone going by first names only, suggesting a familiarity and respect that goes beyond fame and preconceived notions of the type of man or situation that requires a suit.

It's kente but not as you know it: Sauvage goes back to Ghana to put his own spin on the traditional cloth.

For his 2011 collection Black Volta, he drew on his African heritage and worked with a kente weaver in Ghana to come up with his own take on the indigenous fabric. His muted monochrome kente furnished his key look, a double-breasted silk tuxedo with peak lapels and jetted pockets, with an authentic, contemporary spirit. The range's red, white and black colour scheme was taken from the colours of the Black Volta river flag.

He took the collection to Accra and Cape Coast to continue his photography project. 'I wanted to do something with integrity and show my family and friends in Ghana what I was up to, so I got them to model it.' His father arranged a casting to which most of the men in his community turned up, including characters such as Uncle Mac. 'He is one of the oldest men in town. He looks after the cathedral and likes to get drunk and roll around from time to time. He's charming.'

Sauvage is adding womenswear to the range, making a new film called *Costumier* and opening a London flagship store just off Bond Street. Whatever the endeavour, though, his guiding light is always Yves Saint Laurent. 'When I get into a creative quandary, I simply ask myself: "What would Yves do?" He did it all during his career, and he loved Africa. He set the standard I judge my work by.'

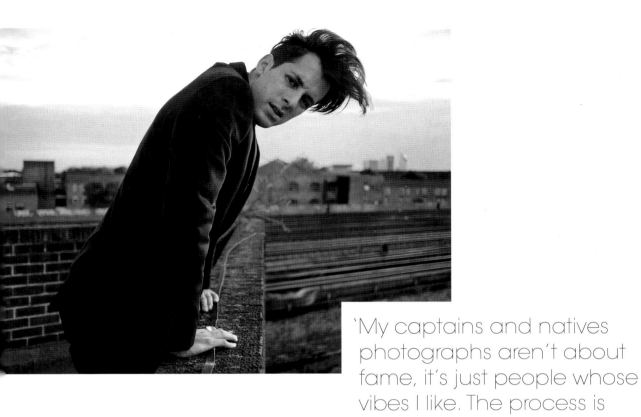

'My captains and natives photographs aren't about fame, it's just people whose vibes I like. The process is organic and natural.'

Straight Talker

THULA SINDI

Thula Sindi's first name means 'quiet' in Xhosa. His parents chose it because he was such a serene baby. But he's certainly learnt to speak up for himself since then and doesn't mince his words when it comes to talking about South African fashion. He grew up in Klerksdorp and attended the National School of Arts in Johannesburg and then the London International School of Fashion. On graduating in 2003 he worked for Vlisco and then Gavin Rajah. He made his label debut in 2006 at South Africa Fashion Week and has since shown in Lagos, Beijing, Luanda, Nairobi, New York, Cotonou, Abu Dhabi, Monaco and Niamey.

On his debut collection for Autumn/Winter 2006/07

The media and the audience largely ignored me. I was crushed because I felt the collection was so right. Charming hand-crochet detailing and brocade tailoring gave the collection a folkloric feel and my first caftan, worn by Millen Magese, closed the show. But nothing. Then one earnest and unforgettable post-show compliment from [SA socialite] Edith Venter changed everything. A week later I had sold every piece 10 times over. It was a real eureka moment.

On his customer

She is independent and shops with a curator's precision and she selects investment pieces with her head and her heart. She is unequivocally purposeful and sophisticated and requires clothing to work for her, not the other way round.

On his design heritage

South Africa's shared urban culture has evolved way past clichés and our fashion design, like every other aspect of our daily lives, is now globally relevant. Modernity isn't the preserve of the West. Everyone can contribute, so we as Africans need to let our cultures grow and steer clear from concepts of tribalism that the West demands to see and appropriates over and over again. My clothes focus on fabric, colour, proportion and execution. That's what good fashion design is about.

On Autumn/Winter 2011/12 – A Woman of Consequence: Part 3

The conclusion of my three-part series conjures up a dream-like funeral procession of impeccably dressed mourners paying homage to the designer who has just left this mortal coil. A sombre palette of black, white and grey is punctuated with blues and polka dots. Yet instead of a lament this collection is a celebration which reaches a crescendo of the most poetically executed evening dresses in silk satin.

LA LESSO

Beach
Babes

Olivia Kennaway and Alice Heusser span Kenya and South Africa with their eco label LaLesso. Kennaway grew up in Mombasa and Nairobi, Heusser in Bath, UK, and Cape Town, and the pair met at Cape Peninsula University of Technology in 2004. They took a road trip to Lamu on the north coast of Kenya one summer, bought up an abundance of vintage kangas and made some handkerchief skirts out of them. Friends back in Cape Town loved them, demand grew and by 2007 LaLesso (lesso is another word for kanga) had become a going concern.

The East African fabric, featuring colourful designs and Swahili aphorisms, is the essence of the brand. 'Olivia has been surrounded and wrapped in kangas since birth and on that first trip to Kenya I fell in love with them', says Heusser. 'It is unlike any other textile. The colours are vibrant and the witty sayings are often cryptic so people translate them completely differently, which is part of their charm.' Like New York brand Suno, LaLesso began sourcing kangas in Kenya but now design their own in order to have more control over efficacy and quality, and broaden their fabrication from cotton to silk, chiffon and viscose.

Also driven by a desire to create an ethical fashion brand, they set up their own workshop in Mombasa and took on several tailors full time. It has grown to become an independent, charity-based production unit called SOKO and is utilised by several brands including ASOS Africa. Having shown in South Africa, Nairobi and Angola, and now selling worldwide, the duo have won awards for their fair trade, carbon-neutral practices.

'Our design philosophy is one of comfort and ease. We want people to feel like they have stepped into another world when they wear LaLesso', says Heusser of their soft and summery pieces. 'The ethereal movements of the sea inspired Spring/Summer 2011. And for Spring/Summer 2012 we looked at tropical fish.' Finishing touches for every collection include hand-carved coconut buttons, Masai beading and brass works from the Bombolulu Workshop, a project by the Association for the Physically Disabled of Kenya. 'Africa is saturated with talent and possibility so we want to promote that wherever we can.'

Kanga and fair trade practices provide the cornerstones of this Kenya-based South African brand.

Las Gidi
Londoner

ITUEN BASI

Nigerian designer Ituen Basi studied theatre arts under Wole Soyinka at the University of Ife but found herself spending more time making stage costumes than walking the boards. After graduation she specialised in clothing technology at the London College of Fashion, and since 1997 she has established her flair for feminine tailoring and textile development. Basi is best known for transforming local fabrics through her patchwork, plaiting, tassel and colour-blocking techniques, most notably in 2009's Ankara and Beads collection, which won the Most Innovative Designer of the Year award at Africa Fashion Week. She returned to win Emerging Designer of the Year in 2010.

For Autumn/Winter 2011/12 she turned her attention to reinventing adire and ase-oke by combining them with styles that transport the wearer to swinging London. The collection of sheaths, pencil skirts with external pockets, waistcoats and 'Love' T-shirts worn with Perspex heart pendants and scooter helmets could all have tumbled out of the costume department of *The Avengers*. A definite departure for the brand, she took home the Most Creative Designer of the Year award at *ARISE* Magazine Fashion Week – Lagos 2011.

Basi also promotes the Nigerian fashion industry with The Fashion Development Agency, a manufacturing unit and educational facility working with micro fashion businesses.

What first attracted you to Ankara?

Due to the import ban on textiles, I decided it best to work with what was readily available in the market. At first I found Ankara loud, overwhelming and downright intimidating, and I hated the fact that it was not exclusive. But then I buckled down to finding solutions and had fun experimenting with it. The possibilities felt endless and Ankara and Beads ended up taking on a life of its own.

How does African fashion fare internationally?

If defined as talents of African origin, then Yves Saint Laurent and Azzedine Alaïa have paved the way. If defined as designers influenced by the continent, then Kenzo, Cacharel, Jean Paul Gaultier and Dries Van Noten are geniuses. But designers based in Africa are only now beginning to be recognised. A continent of 54 nations banded together by landmass with innumerable religions, cultures, languages and colonial influences can't be said to represent any one thing. Our diversity is our strength and on a creative level, we can compete. But the industry is fragmented, inadequately funded and often lacks technical expertise.

What inspires you?

I admire Issey Miyake and Yohji Yamamoto's ability to unapologetically infuse their creativity with their cultural heritage and in doing so inform the West. I try to do the same. The Cool Britannia movement influences me – Liberty prints, Cath Kidston, Vivienne Westwood, the Union Jack, tartan, full English, fringe theatre, the V&A, daffodils! But in the same spirit I also love the hustle and bustle of Balogun Market, the opulence of buba and iro worn by a street hawker, indigo adire and rubber tree plantations in Cross River – the list goes on.

What are your future plans?

I'm opening a flagship store in Lagos and The Fashion Development Agency will be offering weekend classes and opening a fashion library to support fashion students and emerging designers.

Basi's Autumn/Winter 2011/12 helmets make a road safety announcement about the dangers of riding in okadas in Lagos.

Goddess
of Darkness

SAMANTHA COLE LONDON

Samantha Cole lingers on the darker side of life. Her theatrical, predominantly monochrome collections reflect her passions: Alfred Hitchcock, Tim Burton, film noir, Björk, Gareth Pugh, Alexander McQueen and the gothic arts all play their part in her brooding aesthetic which, when crossed with her interest in architecture and technology, results in acute, structural and dramatic garments that use the body more as an easel than a frame.

Born in Liverpool to Nigerian parents and schooled in Lagos, Cole returned to the UK to study at the London College of Fashion, and interned at Burberry. Her debut collection for Spring/Summer 2009, A Journey of Self Discovery, played with Victorian and Georgian silhouettes in lace, leather and taffeta and was styled with an eye on Mary Quant and *A Clockwork Orange*. Her two successive collections, Warrior and A New Dawn, remained stark, powerful and sobering – Oya meets *Mad Max* for the former, post-modernist buildings for the latter.

'My work is severe and sometimes brooding. I'm not trying to fit into a perfect box.'

Her interest in future fabrics and textile manipulation pushes her proportions and finishes to aggressive extremes. For Autumn/Winter 2011/12, Above And Beneath the Definitive Structure, Cole etched Cubist designs into leather minidresses, created a ripple effect with knitwear, put ribs into velvet bodices and reduced silk frocks to artfully distressed tatters. 'As a designer it's important to have the confidence to be true to your passions, ideas and creativity and under no circumstances allow your voice to be stifled. My work is severe and sometimes brooding, yes, but I'm not trying to fit into a perfect box, or please the masses. Fashion has no limits and must embrace advances in order to stay relevant.'

Her unassailable approach has so far stood her in good stead, with invitations to show in London, Lagos, New York and Johannesburg. She's now expanding into menswear, accessories and a high street line.

HENI
New Romantic

Heni Este-hijzen's calling is to ensure that romance is not dead in South African fashion. Born in Johannesburg, he won an *Elle* magazine bursary to attend the city's progressive London International School of Fashion and graduated top of his class in 2002. The same year he won the Smirnoff Fashion Challenge, giving him the financial backing to start his label, and Levi's sponsored his debut show at South Africa Fashion Week for Spring/Summer 2003.

From his first collection, an ode to Jimi Hendrix and 1970s rock and roll album covers realised in bleached and distressed denim, to his more recent Autumn/Winter 2011/12 offering, which saw him send equestrian vampires down the Joburg Fashion Week catwalk wearing bow blouses and capes with their hands bound in red tape, Heni's outlook could never be described as boring. His experimental approach won him Most Promising Designer at Africa Fashion Week 2009. 'The brand is known for its raw, expressive energy and for its nostalgic designs', he says. 'I respect craftsmanship when it comes to the details and I also like to keep things simple: great design, good fabric, incredible fit and spectacular textures.'

Each season tells a narrative with a historical era, moment or figure at its nucleus – the opulence of old Persia expressed through vintage furs and tapestries or imaginary colonial explorers draped in kente cloth are two examples. The results are tender yet resonate in South Africa's complex, multi-ethnic society. 'My best resource and inspiration is Africa and our textiles. I am influenced by the ancestral costumes of our local tribes and reinterpret them into European silhouettes. A lot of people are not aware that we have so many different cultures in the rainbow nation', he says. 'I am proud to be a South African designer. The industry is still a toddler starting to walk but running and even flying is inevitable.'

BESTOW ELAN

Karma
Chameleon

Erzumah Ackerson was born in south London, where 'this land called Ghana' her family would talk about seemed far removed from her own existence. 'It sounded so exotic but I knew it would have significance to me one day', she says.

She began customising her clothes as a teenager – draping gold cord over jackets and adding lace to blouses – and later interned with London Fashion Week designers Jonathan Saunders and Kisa. By the time she established Bestow Elan in 2007, Ackerson's curiosity about her heritage had got the better of her. 'The first collection, Rich in Paradise, was my vision of what Africa would be in an unadulterated state – vibrant in colour, abounding in texture and filled with stylish, confident women.'

She was selected for Kulture2Couture, a show for emerging black designers at the Victoria & Albert Museum, London, and successive collections including Martyr, My Cherie and Liberty have deepened her fascination with simplicity of form, angular draping, embroidery and African prints. 'I spent most of my early years trying to evade the "African designer" title. Now my mission is to create a brand that will be recognised in Ghana and the rest of the continent, and help reeducate people about Africa's creative potential.'

Ackerson's first opportunity to show in Africa came at *ARISE* Magazine Fashion Week – Lagos 2011 with her Autumn/Winter 2011/12 collection, The Silence is Deafening. Epaulette shoulders dominated jumpsuits and party dresses. Necklines plunged and twisted at the front and rose up like crescent moons at the back while hemlines formed trains or petal shapes. Pink animal-print jersey and green-leaf motif Ankara complemented silks in block shades of burgundy, gold, teal, coral and aquamarine. In a word: exotic.

'I believe in dressing to impress. Men should look sharp and desirable every day, not just for special occasions', says Angelo Van Mol, who sets out his style agenda as cleanly and clearly as the cut of one of his white shirts. 'I choose to use only the best materials because the man I design for lives in a luxury world and likes to make an impression.'

Born in Antwerp to a Belgian father and a Ghanaian mother, he developed a respect for impeccable craftsmanship during his studies at the city's Royal Academy of Fine Arts. In his second year he was presented with the Motivation Prize by Ann Demeulemeester for his Imperial Farming collection, while his third-year project, We Are, won the Cocodrilo award.

His 2010 final-year collection, Fade to Black, surveyed mod culture, macho sportswear and the portrait style of art deco artist Tamara de Lempicka, who preferred suave socialites as her subject-matter. Classic shapes such as a leather duffel coat, a cashmere smoking jacket, a cotton shirt with sheer overlay and tailored trousers came in nightfall shades of grey, green, navy, white and black. But what takes the collection to the next level is Van Mol's hand embroidery and embellishments, which formed sequinned and sparkling architectural arch designs across key pieces. The final touch? His handmade patent lace-ups, camel brogues and python Chelsea boots with zips up the back and alcoves carved out of heels and shot through with steel pins.

He showed an updated version of the collection at *ARISE* Magazine Fashion Week – Lagos 2011, where he won the Best Menswear award. As a result, he's found backing for the brand and been invited to show in Amsterdam, London and New York, where he hopes his aesthetic, as much inspired by the Antwerp Six as by Ozwald Boateng, will continue to be well received. 'I've never seen myself as completely Belgian or Ghanaian, but a mix of both, and that's what makes my work special. I also love how big fashion houses use African crafts and turn them into something European – Dries Van Noten does it best – and I can't see the trend disappearing any time soon.'

Antwerp One

ANGELO VAN MOL

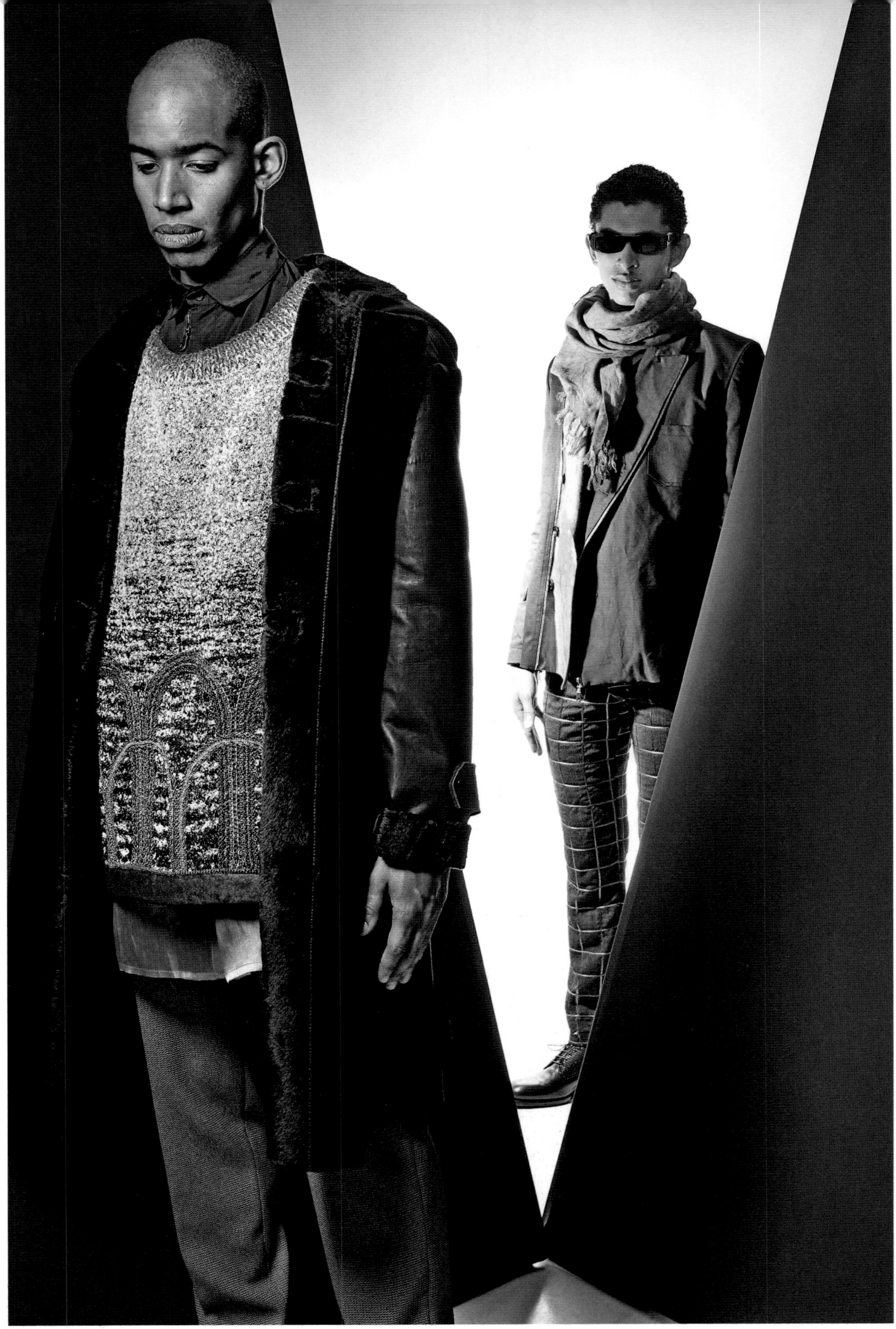

Inspirations as diverse as Napoleon, Tibet, farming, art deco and sportswear have all found their way into Angelo Van Mol's menswear.

It all began with a sewing machine. Aisha Obuobi's grandmother was a seamstress so she grew up surrounded by piles of lustrous African prints and listening to the whir of sewing needles. 'Early on I learnt to appreciate the wonders of creativity and bewitching design and revelled in creating outfits for my favourite dolls', recalls the Accra-based designer. She moved on to customising her own wardrobe and, after studying fashion under Ghanaian designer Joyce Ababio, she introduced Christie Brown in 2008. Fittingly, the label is named in honour of her grandmother.

Obuobi showed her first collection of African-print cocktail dresses at Africa Fashion Week 2009 in Johannesburg, where she won the Emerging Designer of the Year award, and has since participated in *ARISE* shows in Paris and Lagos as well as Canoe and Vlisco shows in Accra. *Destiny's Child* singer Michelle Williams has endorsed the designer by wearing one of her outfits and magazines including *Marie Claire* and *Grazia* have sung her praises.

Her Spring/Summer 2011 collection added Chantilly lace, chiffon, silk and bright block-colour cottons to the African prints she's best known for to create a range of classic maxi dresses, pencil skirts and swing coats accented by fringing, feathers and clusters of covered buttons. For Autumn/Winter 2011/12 her 1940s-inspired range of fitted and full styles, which included hot pants, sleeveless tops with Peter Pan collars and empire-line dresses, were awash with stripes, dots and ribbons. The addition of a range of statement jewellery expands the line further. 'I find beauty in simplicity and appreciate the grace of effortless style', she says. 'I believe in creating ladylike, wearable designs that make my clients feel confident.'

Lady Grace

CHRISTIE BROWN

PIERRE-ANTOINE VETTORELLO

Firestarter

'My name is Italian, my mother is French, my father is Ivorian and I studied in Belgium. I like this complexity of cultures, it has developed my curiosity and allows me to be an explorer without borders', says Pierre-Antoine Vettorello. 'My designs express my vision of the world today. To appreciate African fashion you also have to see its global potential.'

Vettorello was born in Bordeaux, France, in 1985, and studied textiles at the École Nationale Supérieure des Arts Appliqués et des Métiers d'Art in Paris. He has interned at Karl Lagerfeld and Balenciaga and followed in the footsteps of his hero Martin Margiela by entering the masters course at the Royal Academy of Fine Arts, Antwerp. It's here that he developed an aggressive design philosophy. 'My clothes are sexual, organic, graphic – they have to give some emotions, otherwise why make them?'

His 2010 graduate collection Light Me Up drew on two themes. The first were his travels around Africa, specifically Côte d'Ivoire, where he enlisted local craftsmen to carve wooden rib- and breast-shaped body harnesses that were worn like nature's armour. The second was a recurring idea he had of a woman on fire. 'This sounds very dramatic but for a year this image of a woman burning up would keep coming to me like a ghost. She was burning to exist, to express her femininity and her beauty.'

A mottled fire print in shades of grey, yellow, orange and red combusted across silk caftans, blouses and pencil skirts. Feathers engulfed dramatic evening gowns and trench coats. A black mesh body suit and wool blazer were encrusted with ember-like beading and embroidery, and shredded shirts and knitwear resembled what remains after a pyromaniac has done his worst. Worn with the wooden carvings, the look was ferocious and secured him a place at the *ARISE* show at New York Fashion Week for Spring/Summer 2012.

He now collaborates with his ex-classmate Félix Godefroy. The two share an atelier in Brussels but return to Côte d'Ivoire to research their designs. 'African designers are exploring issues that everyone is going to face in the future. We are creating something fresh, passionate and conceptual and also having some fun.'

Sexual, organic, graphic, aggressive: all words the designer uses to describe his no-boundaries womenswear.

'Our aim has always been to create that gasp moment when you see something that is so stunning it takes your breath away', says Malcolm Klûk, one half of KLûK CGDT alongside Christiaan Gabriel Du Toit. 'For us it's not about being fashionable or edgy, it's about celebrating beauty. We want every piece to be special and for our shows to be luxurious and opulent.'

It was mission accomplished for their epic Autumn/Winter 2011/12 show at *ARISE* Magazine Fashion Week – Lagos 2011, which took the audience on a decadent flight of fantasy through Baroque (florals, damask), the Middle East (vintage tapestries from Afghanistan found in a bazaar and sewn onto duchess silk), the Far East (gold and black Indian organza) and Africa (aso-ebi, leopard prints), before finally delivering them up the aisle with a parade of wedding dresses. The collection of capes, shift dresses, high-waisted trousers and floor-length gowns won a place at the *ARISE* New York Fashion Week show for Spring/Summer 2012, as well as the Designer of the Year award.

Klûk was born in Durban and did his MA at London's Central Saint Martins. He remembers an internship at John Galliano in 1989 fondly. 'Amanda Harlech was the stylist, Steven Robinson was the assistant, Julie Verhoeven was sketching the collections, Jasper Conran was the boyfriend and Kate Moss was the fitting model. John was going to show in Paris for the first time and allowing Kate to walk, even though everyone said she was too short for catwalk. Philip Treacy didn't finish the hats in time so it was up to me to dip the ombre silk chiffon in gelatine and drape them for the show.'

KLÛK
CGDT Best Men

He returned to South Africa in 1992 and worked as a fashion forecaster, designer for Jenni Button and fashion editor of *Cosmopolitan* magazine, starting his solo label, Klûk, in 2000. Du Toit grew up in Worcester in the Western Cape and studied at the Cape Technikon Fashion School, where he was awarded Most Promising Designer in 2001. He started CGDT in 2002 and after meeting at a fashion show, the pair opened a store together in 2003.

They announced the marriage of the two labels at Cape Town Fashion Week in 2005 with a wedding-themed show inspired by Christian Dior and the golden age of haute couture. To this day bridalwear remains key to both the brand and their rose-tinted vision of the KLûK CGDT woman. They make six collections a year as well as running a made-to-measure service from their two velvet-clad and scent-laden boutiques in Johannesburg and Cape Town. They've shown in Paris, New York, Moscow, Singapore, Sweden and Mumbai and dressed celebrities including Charlize Theron, Shakira, Annie Lennox, Beyoncé and Rachel Weisz.

Although their outlook is international, Du Toit insists that their hearts will always belong to home. 'There is a long tradition of dressmaking in South Africa and although a lot of the old skills and luxury fabrics are hard to find, the vibe here is great. Out of a new country comes optimism and we believe we are one of the new frontiers of fashion returning to more homespun and individual aesthetics.'

'Our aim is to create that gasp moment when you see something that is so stunning that it takes your breath away.'

FACES

Kinée Diouf is no blank canvas. Her idiosyncratic prowl and determined facial expression that borders on a growl makes her one of a kind on the catwalk and puts new meaning into the overused term 'supermodel'. 'She's quite brilliant in a very ethnic way. What I like about her is her model attitude. She could be someone's muse because of her style and the way she walks on the runway', enthuses model campaigner Bethann Hardison. 'At the *ARISE* show at New York Fashion Week she was lucky enough to come out just as the music hit and she was on point, she exuded energy. For us in the industry, it's important that girls get a chance to shine like that. She's the one I follow.'

The Senegalese model first came onto the scene in 2006 when she appeared in the Givenchy and Vivienne Westwood shows in Paris. She is now based in New York and has walked for several major fashion houses and African designers including Lanvin, Louis Vuitton, Yves Saint Laurent, Jewel by Lisa, Duro Olowu and Ere Dappa. She's done campaigns for Gap, Benetton and MAC and her magazine covers include *French*, *Trace*, *Tank Magazine* and *ARISE*.

Super Model

KINÉE DIOUF

Diouf fans Juergen Teller and Duro Olowu took her to Greece in 2008 to shoot this Yves Saint Laurent story for *Tank*.

ALEK WEK

Model Citizen

Alek Wek was born into the southern Sudanese Dinka tribe in 1977. She moved to London in 1991 to escape civil war, where her mother and three siblings later joined her. Her father perished in the war. In 1995 Wek was studying art when a scout spotted her. 'I tried modelling for six months but wasn't getting any work. Then I went to New York for castings and found an agent who wanted to see me grow and give me space to become a woman. That's when I realised I could be myself and didn't have to do any project, shoot or job that I didn't feel comfortable with', she told *ARISE* magazine.

As a dark-skinned African model she found many doors closed to her at first, but with success came confidence. 'All these people who said I was strange were suddenly interested once I'd done a shoot with Steven Meisel, was opening all the shows in New York and shot for Italian *Vogue*. I was still the same girl but now

I had the stamp of approval. Then after that, they all wanted Alek look-alikes. But there are no Alek look-alikes. It's our differences that make us beautiful.'

Her 2007 memoir, *Alek: Sudanese Refugee to International Supermodel*, discusses her modelling experiences in an effort to empower young girls. She was the first African model to appear on the cover of *Elle* in 1997 and her campaigns, catwalk appearances and covers are too many to mention. Wek is also a member of the US Committee for Refugees' Advisory Council and speaks on behalf of Doctors Without Borders. Plus her own initiative WEK (Working to Educate Kids) builds schools and offers scholarships. 'The most amazing thing that fashion has given me is the opportunity to give a voice to the voiceless. Since I was a refugee, I can shed a light on our responsibility to educate our young ones and tell them it's okay to have beliefs and that hard work does pay off.'

She also has the handbag label Wek 1933, which is dedicated to her father, and has designed diamond jewellery for De Beers. 'Lately I've been modelling in moderation to work on these other projects and do things I truly believe in.'

Wek's singular good looks caused a seismic shift in the model industry when she rose to fame in the late 1990s.

Candice Swanepoel, Behati Prinsloo and Heidi Verster represent a different face of African beauty. They might look like all-American girls but are in fact from South Africa, and proudly so. Candice was discovered in a flea market in Durban aged 16. Little did she know then that a few years later she'd have shot with Mario Testino for *V* magazine, with Steven Meisel for a *Vogue Italia* cover and with Bruce Webber for French *Vogue* alongside Brooke Shields. Boys will know her best, though, as a Victoria's Secret Angel.

Candice Swanepoel, Behati Prinsloo and Heidi Verster

UNDERCOVER AGENTS

Behati was born in South Africa but grew up in Namibia. She was signed up by Storm's Sarah Doukas (who discovered Kate Moss in the 1990s) and is currently in demand from a range of clients including *i-D*, *V*, Prada, Paul Smith and Versace. She's also a Victoria's Secret Angel and designs a bikini range for the brand as well as being one of its ridiculously sexy ambassadors.

Heidi grew up in Port Elizabeth and moved to New York to model at the age of 18. She's been on the cover of *French* and *The Block*, done campaigns for Tommy Hilfiger, Diesel and Dolce & Gabbana and walked for Issey Miyake, Alexander Wang and Cushnie et Ochs, to name just a few.

All three were shot by Daniela Midenge for the May 2010 cover of *SA Marie Claire* wearing Nigerian designer Deola Sagoe. They've also supported South African-based designers Black Coffee and Loin Cloth & Ashes by modelling for them at the *ARISE* New York Fashion Week show.

ARMANDO CABRAL

Sole Man

Armando Cabral is a man of many talents. He was born in Guinea-Bissau and grew up in Lisbon, where one day in 2001 he followed his sister to her modelling agency. He was signed up on the spot. He moved to London and then to New York in 2006, where his regal good looks and positive attitude have kept him in high demand ever since.

Cabral has been the face of Benetton and Alexander McQueen for Puma, walked for Louis Vuitton, Ozwald Boateng and Dries Van Noten and shot with Mario Testino for *V Man* and with Greg Kadel for *Numéro Homme*. Modelling has taken him to four continents, and on more than one occasion four countries in one week. But his favourite job to date was the 2010 holiday campaign for H&M, shot with younger brother Fernando, who is just beginning to follow in Armando's footsteps. 'It was fun and I was so proud of him', he says. 'Fernando has big potential so I'm behind him all the way.'

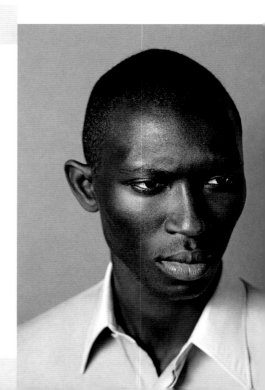

Whether modelling or designing shoes, Cabral always takes a considered and credible approach to his work.

Cabral's latest venture is into shoe design. He began his eponymous line in 2009 in association with Rucky Zambrano (a former creative director at Hugo Boss) and Simon Foxton (fashion director at *i-D*) and it's now sold in Europe, Japan, Angola and the UK. 'I love shoes. For me they sum up a person's taste and should act as the perfect complement to one's lifestyle', he says. 'Through modelling I've learnt a lot about good design and what it takes to have international appeal. I have channelled that into the brand.' His focus is on comfort and craftsmanship – each pair is handmade in Italy – and on giving classic styles such as loafers, sand boots and deck shoes a colourful twist.

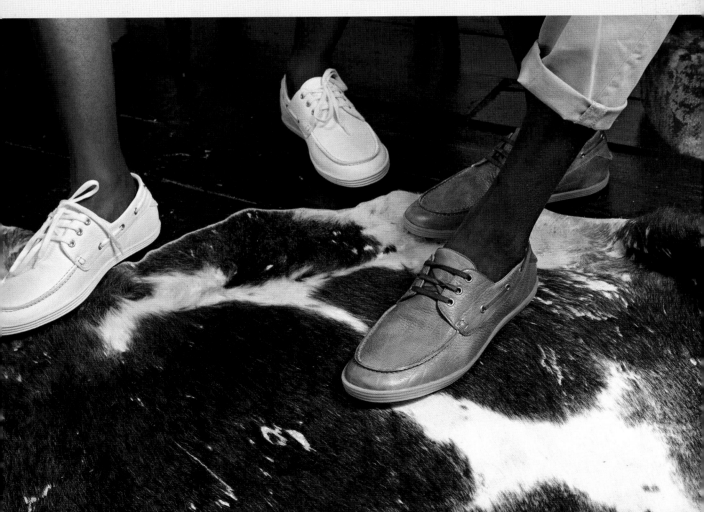

FLAVIANA
MATATA

Beauty pageants are brimming with women claiming to be passionate about philanthropy, but in Flaviana Matata's case, it's true. The former Miss Universe Tanzania works with a number of African charities including the Diamond Empowerment Fund and the Tanzania Mitindo House, and in May 2011 she set up the non-profit Flaviana Matata Foundation in memory of her mother, who died in a boating accident in 1996. 'The organisation will give leaders in health, business, government and communities the opportunity to be part of a movement that helps the most vulnerable in our society – young women and kids', she says.

Born in Shinyanga, she completed a degree in electrical engineering in 2007 and was intending to follow the subject as her career until her friends persuaded her to enter the pageant. She accepted the challenge 'kicking and screaming' and won. She proceeded to represent Tanzania at the Miss Universe final, coming sixth. Her title took her to South Africa, where she began modelling. In 2009 she visited New York to attend a Tanzanian charity event and was spotted by hip hop mogul Russell Simmons. 'He looked at me and said "You're going to be a star." I chuckled, but he meant it.'

Since relocating to New York in 2010, she's done editorials for *Dazed & Confused*, *i-D*, *Nylon*, *ARISE*, *True Love* and *Essence* magazines, campaigns for Topshop and TIGI Hair and walked for Jason Wu, Tommy Hilfiger and Vivienne Westwood. Photographer Nick Knight cast her in his tribute film to Alexander McQueen alongside Ajak Deng, Anais Mali, Jeneil Williams, Joan Smalls, Kinée Diouf and Rose Cordero. And she won Model of the Year at *ARISE* Magazine Fashion Week – Lagos 2011.

Matata believes her no-fuss approach to modelling and decision to keep her head bald helps her to 'represent the majority of black women' and makes her a 'canvas ready for an artist to work on'. Tanzanian designer Anisa Mpungwe of Loin Cloth & Ashes succinctly sums up her appeal: 'I like Flaviana because she's grounded. She has an amazing air of innocence, great poise and piercing eyes.'

Modelling may not have been her initial calling but, like her role model Iman, she is putting the opportunities it has given her to good use. 'Iman was a pioneer who opened doors for many African models and despite her massive success, she remains a true sister from Africa.' So too, no doubt, will Matata.

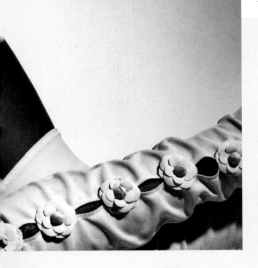

From designers such as Xuly Bët and Chris Seydou, to its tailor-made street style captured by photographers Malick Sidibé and Seydou Keïta, Bamako is a city steeped in fashion. The Malian capital is also where Nana Keita grew up wanting to be a model. 'I was obsessed with the gorgeous women who used to do the L'Oréal commercials and would spend a lot of time in front of the mirror practicing my best "Because I'm worth it!" I even had different accents depending on the woman I was channelling', she says. Keita moved to New York for university and began modelling in 2008. She's since walked for Lanvin, Martin Grant, Manish Arora, Suno, Vivienne Westwood, Rick Owens and St John.

What were your first impressions of the US?
I found there to be ignorance about Africa because of how the media portrays our continent. I hope people in the West can educate themselves enough to understand that Africa is not a country and it's not all misery and civil wars.

What have been your career highlights so far?
Avon was the first job when I realised models could make money! But I will always remember the first *ARISE* show at Bryant Park in February 2009. I shared the runway with Grace Jones, Liya Kibede, Alek Wek and Tyson Beckford and also had the privilege of walking for Xuly Bët.

What is your X factor?
In my country they say: 'The honey doesn't state its own sweetness.' What I will say, though, is that everything I do is with passion and dedication and that I always strive to stay true to my culture and my religion.

What is in your wardrobe?
Tracy Reese, Isaac Mizrahi, Lanvin, Donna Karan, Gilles Touré, Alphadi and Christian Louboutin.

What are your ambitions?
I want to become a successful model, architect and UN ambassador so that I can help others. It would also be nice if I too could inspire another young lady to want to stand in front of a mirror and imitate me saying, 'Because I'm worth it.'

NANA KEITA

Bamako
Beauty

GER DUANY,
SALIEU JALLOH
AND SY ALLASANE

THE HARLEM BOYS

Ger Duany, Salieu Jalloh and Sy Allasane converged on New York City from different corners of Africa and found favour, and each other, through modelling. Each has a story to tell, yet what unites these three confidants is their interwoven immigrant experience as part of the pan-African aggregation in the city that never sleeps.

'We all met while doing shows and as Africans we naturally gravitated together. We'd always talk to each other about our childhoods back in the motherland', says Duany. His story began in Akobo, Sudan, where he grew up amid civil war and became a child soldier in the Sudanese People's Liberation Army. He moved between refugee camps in Ethiopia and Kenya, and was resettled to the United States in 1994 aged 16. He won a basketball scholarship to college and then began acting. He starred in the 2004 film *I Heart Huckabees* and was introduced to modelling by Tyson Beckford. His clients have included *The Fader*, *Numéro Homme*, Sean John, *ARISE* and Nom de Guerre. In January 2011 Duany returned home to vote in the referendum on the secession of south Sudan and was reunited with his family for the first time in 18 years. Kenyan director Wanuri Kahiu documented his trip for the film *Ger: To Be Separate*. 'It's a story of endurance and the power of love. My message to the world is to stand up for what you believe in', he says. 'When I am on a runway now, I am representing the Republic of South Sudan and the entire continent.'

Duany met Allasane at an Andrew Buckler show and they lived together for a short time in Harlem. In 2010 they were both cast in Andrew Dosunmu's Sundance-selected film *Restless City*. The story focuses on Allasane's character Djibril, a Senegalese immigrant and frustrated musician who hustles on Canal Street. In real life, Allasane was born in Mauritania in 1982 but was deported to Senegal by the UN to avoid genocide in 1989. From here he went to Côte d'Ivoire, Paris, London and finally New York in 2005, where he began modelling. He's worked with Benetton, 3.1 Phillip Lim, Yigal Azrouël, *Vibe* and *ARISE*. 'Modelling made me realise that I had a part to play in the African renaissance and awoke the pan-Africanist inside of me', Allasane says. *Restless City* only confirmed these sentiments. 'There is a little bit of Djbril in me. His story is that of every African immigrant in New York and it made me feel homesick so after filming I came back to Dakar.'

Allasane met Jalloh at a Sean John fashion show, where they bonded as fellow Fulanis. Jalloh hails from Sierra Leone and moved to the United States at the age of 13. He began modelling in New York in 2008 and his star rose quickly, with clients including Benetton, Victor Glemaud, Richard Chai, Rag & Bone, Tommy Hilfiger, *Vogue Hommes Japan*, *Dansk*, *GQ*, *Wonderland*, *ARISE* and *Client*. He also took part in the 2010 BET TV show *Model City*. 'I see modelling as an opportunity to show the world that we can all get along no matter where we're from. Unity is what we need', says Jalloh. In the future he hopes to establish an arts programme for children in Sierra Leone.

FACES OF AFRICA

OLUCHI ONWAEGBA

In 1998 Oluchi Onweagba won the inaugural M-Net *Face of Africa* continent-wide model search. The 17-year-old Lagosian fended off entrants from 19 countries to take the crown for Nigeria on the South African TV network show and received a contract from Elite Model Management. She relocated to New York and within a year she had been on the cover of *Vogue Italia* and shot with Steven Meisel for US *Vogue*. She went on to forge the most successful career in the competition's history. She's been on the cover of *i-D*, *Surface*, *ARISE*, *Clam*, *Elle* and *True Love*, fronted campaigns for L'Oréal, Clinique, GAP, H&M and Victoria's Secret and walked for John Galliano, Ralph Lauren, Christian Dior, Chanel, Donna Karan and Giorgio Armani.

Oluchi (meaning 'work of God' in Ibo) put her business degree from New York University to good use by setting up the modelling agency O Model Africa in conjunction with the Shine Group in Johannesburg in 2007, which has provided *Face of Africa* alumni such as Kate Tachie-Menson and Lukundo Nalungwe with modelling contracts.

Do you feel pride in representing African beauty internationally?

From the moment I won *Face of Africa*, I felt that I had a responsibility to myself and to Africa to have a good career. That has been my driving force. I didn't want to let myself down, or the continent down.

In what ways do you support the African fashion industry?

O Model Africa is my way of opening doors for other young African beauties. It feels good to know there are more African models now. I have also walked in several fashion weeks in both South Africa and Nigeria through the years. I've always longed for African fashion to grow and now it's getting there. The industry's success promotes positive messages about Africa's cultural and economical progress. I live in a Western society where very little good information about my beloved Africa is available so it's our responsibility as Africans to make change happen.

Which African fashion brands do you wear?

Deola Sagoe for when I want to feel like a goddess, Tiffany Amber for elegant and effortless glamour, Jewel by Lisa for casual chic and Sun Goddess for the way it embraces my continent. I also admire Stoned Cherrie, Bongiwe Walaza, Duro Olowu, Lola Faturoti, Chris Aire and Zizi Cardow – they all blow me away.

Will the resurgence in black models working internationally be long-lasting?

I knew 10 years ago that there would be a shift. There were so many stunning girls from across Africa and nations such as Haiti and Jamaica waiting to be discovered and now that they have they can't be denied the opportunities that rightfully belong to them.

KATE TACHIE-MENSON

The 2008 M-Net *Face of Africa* winner hails from Accra, Ghana, where she began her modelling career. She's appeared in SA *Elle*, *Glamour* and *Cosmopolitan* and walked in Cape Town, Joburg, Mozambique, Tanzania and Angola fashion weeks. She currently divides her time between London and New York. 'African catwalks are quite different from the European ones. Models are more relaxed and you don't have to be a size zero in order to participate. Also the collections showcased by my favourite designers such as Art Dress by Kofi Ansah exhibit the diversity of our cultures', she says. 'Iman, Oluchi and Anna Getaneh paved the way for me. Now the sky is the limit.'

LUKUNDO NALUNGWE

In 2010 Lukundo Nalungwe became the first Zambian to
win M-Net *Face of Africa*. Her road has not been easy. Her
mother died when she was 11, her father when she was 18,
and her brother passed away the day before the competition
casting. She now sees her victory as not simply her own. 'It
made my family proud and my country proud. Winning
was the greatest feeling ever.' A week after the Lagos final,
she made her international catwalk debut at the *ARISE*
New York Fashion Week show. Her first campaign was for
Woolworths and she's appeared in SA *Cosmopolitan*, *Elle*,
Marie Clare, *Fair Lady* and *O, The Oprah Magazine*.

Man About Town

DAVID AGBODJI

Calvin Klein muse, artist, photographer and model of the moment; here is David Agbodji in his own words.

'My family is from Togo but me and my siblings grew up all over the place (mostly in Moscow and New York). The moving didn't help much with making friends, but I was very into sports and art so it was easy. For as far as I can remember I was planning to become some kind of artist (I think either an oil painter or graphic designer). Everybody in my family can draw so we were encouraged to do a lot of art. In fact my father used to "purchase" our artwork, so every time we needed extra cash we would scrape up some drawings. And then the modelling thing happened on its own and I just rode the wave. And modelling got me interested in photography, as cliché as that sounds. What's funny is that I used to really hate photography and hardly considered it serious art. The thing that got me into it was the fact that I couldn't understand how it took certain photographers so long to do something that I thought, at the time, was so simple. Eventually I just had to satisfy my curiosity and fell in love with the medium in the process. Now I realise how hard a medium it is. It even made me appreciate modelling more in turn. I don't really plan much so I'm not sure what's next. For all I know I might just get bored of photography as fast as I fell in love and move on to something else. But right now it's my passion and I can't stop thinking of random stuff I wanna create so I'll just have fun for the moment. People usually ask me why I've called my photo website Heart of Bull, but it's simply the translation of my last name, Agbodji. Here is some of my work.'

Ouagadougou Girl

GEORGIE BADDIEL

This self-confessed 'tomboy' was born into a big family in Abidjan, Côte d'Ivoire, and grew up in Burkina Faso, where she began to pursue modelling at the age of 14 to pay her school fees. She won Miss Burkina Faso, was crowned Miss Africa in 2005 and then moved to Europe. Now New York-based, she's walked for Louis Vuitton, Lanvin, Giles, Diane von Furstenberg, Halston, Korto Momolu, Jewel by Lisa, KLûK CGDT and Marc Jacobs, and graced the pages of *Pop*, *Interview*, *ARISE*, *i-D*, *Harper's Bazaar* and *Vogue Italia*, to name just a few.

What are your views on African fashion?
I believe that African fashion has a future, which is why I support and participate in African fashion weeks, designer shows and photo shoots. Our continent also has amazing textiles; my favourite is le faso dans fani, which is woven by women in Burkina Faso villages. The raw materials and dyes are all organic and the effort the women put into the quality of the product is remarkable. I wear it all the time in order to promote it and give a better life to those who make it.

What is your X factor?

My Burkina beauty, smile and personality are what get me booked. I aspire to be like Katoucha, who possessed beauty, elegance and a sense of humour.

Is the landscape for black models improving?

There aren't that many top African models so I do carry some obligation to enlighten the world about the amazing fashion and people in Africa. Things are improving though. There are more international designers using us black pearls for their shows and campaigns as a way of attracting a new clientele.

Where are your favourite places in the world?

I love Ouagadougou because it's home. I love Paris for its beautiful and romantic boulevards and London for the street style and architecture. But my first day in New York City I just knew that it was the city where all of my dreams could come true.

What are your ambitions?

I'm designing a lingerie range and will model the campaigns. I also want to create a magazine and keep promoting African designers.

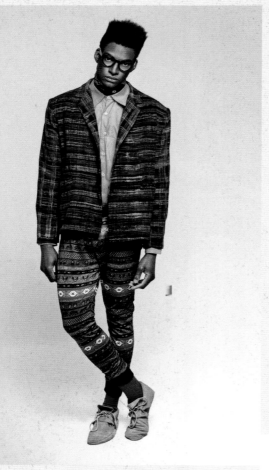

Akintayo Ogunkoya became one to watch when David Sims shot him for a United Colors of Benetton campaign in 2008. The Nigerian model's distinctive cat-like green eyes singled him out as something special and he was selected to walk exclusively for the Dior Autumn/Winter 2008/09 show in his first season out. He's since appeared on catwalks for Versace, Belstaff, Costume National, Hermès, Krizia, DKNY and Etro and his campaigns include Firetrap and DKNY. He's also appeared in editorials for *DANSK*, *GQ* and *Vogue Hommes International* (in which he depicted the late artist Jean-Michel Basquiat) and on the cover of *FAB* magazine. Ty was originally scouted while studying mechanical engineering at Imperial College London and remains based in the city, where he's also pursing his musical interests as part of the duo Rockstar and Swagger. If his eyes are closed you'll recognise him by his messy Afro and a tattoo of Romans 8.31 on his left arm.

Bright Eyes

TY OGUNKOYA

Fabulous Two

ATAUI DENG & AJAK DENG

Ajak Deng and Ataui Deng (no relation but firm friends) are leading the way in the Sudanese takeover of the international catwalks. Alongside budding models Atong Arjok, Ayor Makur Chuot, Akuol de Mabior and Abul Akol, these dark-skinned beauties are forging careers in the mould of Alek Wek's success in the 1990s.

Ataui (whose aunt happens to be Wek) was born in Khartoum but her family fled to San Antonio, Texas, in 2004, to avoid the protracted civil war. She was scouted in 2008 and within two weeks she was working at New York Fashion Week. 'It all seemed to happen overnight. I did 16 shows in my first season – Jeremy Laing, L'Wren Scott, Proenza Schouler, Zac Posen – it was like a dream', she says. Her clients have since included Kenzo, Christian Dior, John Galliano, Macy's, V and *Harper's Bazaar*.

Ajak (real name Angelique) was born in Tong and likewise left Sudan due to civil unrest. Her family relocated first to a refugee camp in Kakuma, Kenya, and then to Australia, where she began modelling in Melbourne. Since arriving in New York in 2009 her rise has been nothing short of stratospheric. Her covers include *Pop'Africana* and *i-D*, her campaigns include Topshop and Benetton and her catwalk gigs are prodigious. 'It's hard being a black model but we can turn the impossible into the possible', she told *Vogue Black*.

Ajak and Ataui caused a fashion blog sensation when they appeared together in an editorial for *ARISE* magazine (Le Rendezvous, issue 11) in which Ataui playfully nibbled Ajak's ear, and they often share the same catwalk. A stand-out moment came in October 2010, when they formed part of what industry insiders dubbed the 'Fabulous Five', closing Lanvin's Spring/Summer 2011 show alongside Jeneil Williams, Melodie Monrose and Jourdan Dunn. Each wore a tropical leaf-print all-in-one and butterfly belt from the gladiator-inspired collection. 'It was a powerful moment for all of us. There was a unique unity that captivated everyone in attendance. Alber Elbaz is a genius and a pleasure to work with', says Ataui.

RUE
COPERNIC

ART

Fine Dandy

KARL-
EDWIN
GUERRE

Since 2008, Karl-Edwin Guerre has been photographing the sartorially superior in his native New York and beyond for his street style blog Guerreisms (originally Swagger360). Among them are many devilishly dressed Afropolitans such as *Ghubar* magazine editor Mboko Ndimba Mobutu, Ozwald Boateng designer Sam Lambert and artist Shaka Maidoh.

'I wanted to share with the public looks that go beyond fashion', he says of his vision, which bypasses trend-obsessed hipsters in favour of modern-day Renaissance men and women. He pays special attention to shoes, accessories and details. 'My subjects are dressed in such a way that exudes respect for themselves and their peers. I find that it's the people that dress with a fun, rebellious attitude that make me smile. I especially love the way that Africans living abroad mix traditional attire with European-inspired clothing. I like to call them the Young and Fly.'

Guerre has become a dapperly dressed fixture at New York and Paris fashion weeks, where he often captures African models such as Sudanese beauty Ajak Deng dashing between shows. 'They come from a different place, a different mindset, and I can't help but believe that this comes across in front of the lens. It gives these girls that "it" factor.'

His 2010 exhibition at W Hotel Times Square, The Dandies: Gentlemen of Nonchalant Elegance and Effortless Style, featured refined men from around the world and his future plans include a book and travel to Africa.

'Ghubar's Ndimba Mobutu is creating a splash in terms of his dress sense. He never goes over the top but has become the subject of many street style photographers.'

Congolese sapeur Jocelyn Armel is nicknamed Le Bachelor. Guerre makes a pilgrimage to his Connivences menswear boutique every time he's in Paris. 'He's one of those gentlemen that never gets it wrong', he says.

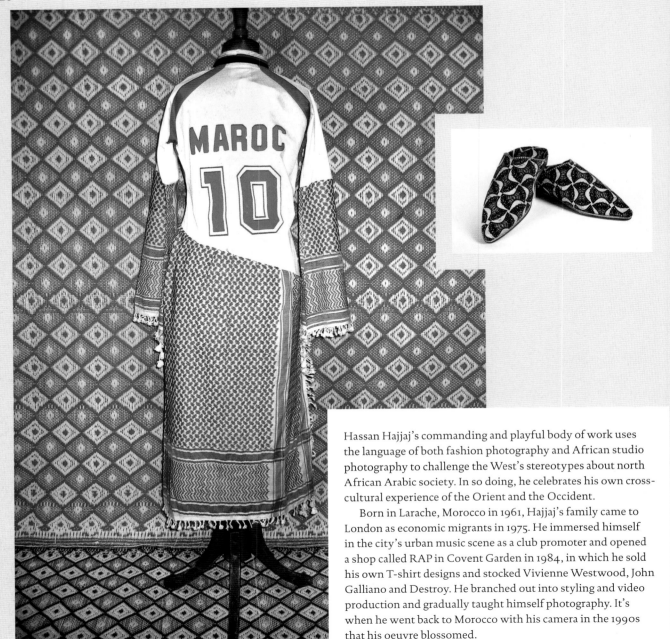

Hassan Hajjaj's commanding and playful body of work uses the language of both fashion photography and African studio photography to challenge the West's stereotypes about north African Arabic society. In so doing, he celebrates his own cross-cultural experience of the Orient and the Occident.

Born in Larache, Morocco in 1961, Hajjaj's family came to London as economic migrants in 1975. He immersed himself in the city's urban music scene as a club promoter and opened a shop called RAP in Covent Garden in 1984, in which he sold his own T-shirt designs and stocked Vivienne Westwood, John Galliano and Destroy. He branched out into styling and video production and gradually taught himself photography. It's when he went back to Morocco with his camera in the 1990s that his oeuvre blossomed.

Arabian Knight

HASSAN HAJJAJ

Hajjaj's images of veiled young women, either on scooters or reclining like odalisques in a Matisse painting, help to demystify the veil and women's status as objects of the gaze. These ladies are far from repressed: they're happily and colourfully attired and stare straight back.

Hajjaj casts from the streets of Marrakech – dancers, Gnawa musicians, souk traders, snake charmers, water sellers, henna girls, friends – and creates portraits depicting suggestive narratives set against ornate backdrops. His subjects wear what at first look like conventional veils, djelabbahs, caftans and babouches, but they are actually covered in counterfeit designer logos or made from perennial fashion fabrics – camouflage, polka dots and leopard print. 'My images are a peep through the keyhole to my culture. I want to show that we're all the same', he says. 'Maybe we dress, eat and speak a little differently, but we all have similar needs and desires.'

He often borrows pop art's reappropriation of well-known brands by framing his photographs in a mosaic of everyday products, further reaffirming the ebb and flow between contemporary consumerism and classical traditions and between life and art. And with studios in London and Marrakech, his work also straddles textile, furniture, graphic and accessory design. His salon installations, which have popped up at galleries, festivals and theatres worldwide, bring everything together and act as interactive social spaces that recreate the hustle and bustle of the souk. 'Morocco is a crossroads between the Mediterranean, Europe and Africa. The young people don't wear traditional clothes any more. Rap fans, indie kids, tourists, nightclubs, MTV – it's all in Morocco now', he says. 'What next? All I can say is, inshallah!'

Happy
Snapper

In 2008 Chris Saunders was one of the first photographers to document the Smarteez, Soweto's answer to Tokyo's Harajuku girls. The style tribe, headed up by Kepi Mngomezulu, Lethabo Tsatsinyane, Floyd Mantoane and Sibu Sithole, took South Africa's reputation as a rainbow nation to its literal extreme with a neon dress code assembled from thrift shops, fabric stores and each others' wardrobes.

Saunders finds the young crew's non-conformist and DIY approach to appearance captivating. 'They are a sterling example of South Africa's new post-apartheid generation', he says. 'They come from humble beginnings, are educated and creative, and see through the racial stereotypes in our society. All they want to do is create beauty and live their art.' He has continued to follow the Smarteez' trajectory and in 2011 they graduated from sidewalk to catwalk with their debut show at SA Fashion Week.

CHRIS SAUNDERS

Saunders has captured street style across South Africa for his fashion blog Team Uncool, and his output also includes film, fashion, reportage and advertising. He's contributed to *Dazed & Confused*, *ARISE*, *GQ*, *Glamour* and *FHM* and spent a year at Benetton's research centre Fabrica in Treviso, Italy, working on *Colors* magazine.

What unifies his work is its instinctual exploration of the dilemmas and possibilities of social diversity in the post-modern African city. His street portraits celebrate individuality and bravery in the face of the urban grind and zooms in on those risktakers who creatively construct their own identities through dress, art and attitude. 'South Africa is a multicultural melting pot of angst, joy and mayhem. In this environment you feel overwhelmed and as if your environment could burn down around you, but at the same time positive and amazing people surround you. I love shooting those who are out of the ordinary and tickle the eccentric side of my brain', he says. 'My country is the epicentre of anthropology in Africa but we still have so much to learn from our African brothers. If more African collaboration happened things would be vastly different on this continent.'

Chris Saunders won the 2010 ACP *Courier* Photo Competition for his image 'Dressed Up'. Taken from his Dance series for *Colors* magazine, it captures Real Actions, a Pantsula dance crew from Orange Farm, South Africa, in a rare moment of rest.

See no evil, hear no evil, speak no evil: Saunders's imagery always celebrates freedom, diversity and positivity.

GLOSSARY
& FURTHER
READING

Adire An indigo cloth produced by the Yoruba women of southwestern Nigeria employing a variety of resist-dye techniques. Adire eleko uses cassava starch paste to create freehand designs applied with a chicken's feather before the cloth is folded and dyed. Adire oniko uses raffia to tie up the cloth before dyeing. There are over 400 designs that most often appear in squares, each with a recognised meaning.

Ankara A richly patterned printed cotton fabric that originated in Turkey and is now mainly made and consumed in Nigeria.

Appliqué A technique of applying ornamentation to fabric using needlework, embroidery, pieces of fabric and trimmings to create designs. A popular art in Benin.

Aso oke Meaning 'top cloth' in English, this is a formal textile that is handwoven by the Yoruba men of southwestern Nigeria using a narrow-strip loom. It's made predominantly from silk and cotton and comes in thin ribbons that are then sewn together.

Agbada / Riga An embroidered flowing robe with wide sleeves and side openings, worn by chiefs and on ceremonial occasions.

Babouches Moroccan leather slippers.

Batik A technique of making printed fabric by creating patterns on both sides of the fabric with wax so that these areas are prevented from absorbing colour when the fabric is dyed. The process is repeated with different wax patterns and coloured dyes to create the final design. The method originated in Indonesia.

Bogolanfini / Bogolan A Malian cotton mud cloth featuring distinctive white and brown designs, created using fermented mud. Originally a ceremonial cloth, Chris Seydou made it fashionable.

Boubou / Bubu A floor-length roomy gown, often elaborately embroidered on the neckline. It's worn by West African women and is testament to the Islamic influence in the region.

Brocade A shuttle-woven textile using a draw loom to create ornamental patterns in the weft of the fabric that appear to be embroidered.

Buba and Iro A tailored blouse and wrapper skirt worn together as a matching outfit by Yoruba women.

Caftan / Kaftan A cloak-like tunic with long sleeves worn across North Africa, similar to a boubou.

Damask A heavy woven fabric with a pattern created with one warp yarn and one weft yarn using silk, wool, linen or cotton. It has a lustrous finish and is commonly used in upholstery.

Dashiki A loose, boxy top worn by Nigerian men that can be worn with an agbada and sokoto (pyjama-like trousers).

Djelabbah A long tunic with a hood, worn in the Maghreb.

Dirac A long, light, diaphanous voile dress, worn by Somalian women.

Fancy An inexpensive printed cloth produced in West Africa, Asia and Europe that looks similar to African wax print, except that the design only appears on one side of the fabric.

Fez A red felt cylindrical hat with a tassel, named after the Moroccan city.

Filigree A delicate metalwork technique using threaded gold or silver to create lace-like patterns. Its roots lie with Egyptian jewellers.

Gele An elaborate Yoruban head tie, usually made from ase-oke, damask, brocade or hayes.

Indigo A dye made from an extract of the leaf of the indigo tree and used to create several West African fabrics, including adire and ndop. Leaves are pounded into a pulp, shaped into balls and dried. To use, they are crushed with ash, stirred into water and left to ferment for three days in dyeing pits.

Kaba / Up and Down A two-piece outfit worn by Ghanaian women. A fitted blouse, often with wide sleeves, and a wrapper skirt. It can also be worn with a matching headwrap.

Kanga A brightly printed cotton fabric from East Africa that features Swahili aphorisms written around the border.

Kente A woven textile using silk and cotton to create a variety of colours and patterns. It comes from the Ashante people of Ghana in the 18th century and was originally worn by royalty.

Kikoi / Kikoy A printed fabric from East Africa usually worn as a sarong.

Kitenge / Chitenge An East African batik-printed fabric featuring political or religious messages.

Lapa A length of brightly printed cotton produced in Liberia and sold in three-lapas lengths (around 5.5 metres). It can be worn and used in many ways.

Pagne / Wrapper An all-purpose term for West African dress, ranging from a single length of cotton cloth wrapped around the body to a more formal three-piece ensemble including a tailored top, wrapped skirt and headwrap.

Sarouel Moroccan trousers with a low crotch and tapered leg.

Shwe Shwe A printed cotton cloth originally developed in England but now made in South Africa that traditionally comes in three colours: blue, red and brown.

Tie Dye A resist-dye method of decorating fabric or a garment by tying string around certain areas in order to prevent dye from being absorbed. The technique is widely used in the Hausa region of Nigeria.

Thoub A fully covering Islamic robe, worn in Sudan.

Turban Intricately tied headscarf worn in Northern Africa as well as the Middle East and Southwest Asia. Turbans have been popularised by fashion.

Wax Hollandais The patented name for real Dutch wax-printed fabric manufactured by Vlisco in the Netherlands but considered an African fabric. The print process is based on batik.

FURTHER READING

Ekua Abuda, *Celebrating Fashion Today* (Essential Interiors Magazine, Lagos, 2010)

ARISE, issues 1–12 (2011)

Ben Arogundade, *Black Beauty: A History and a Celebration* (Thunder's Mouth Press / Pavilion Books Ltd, London, 2000)

Kaat Debo, ed., *Beyond Desire* (Ludion / MoMu, Ghent, 2005)

Angela Fisher, *Africa Adorned* (Harry N. Abrams, New York, 1984)

Bérnice Geoffroy-Schneiter, *Africa Is In Style* (Assouline, New York, 2005)

The Global Africa Project (Museum of Arts and Design / Prestel Publishing / International Women's Society, London, 2010)

Suzanne Gott and Kristyne Loughran, ed., *Contemporary African Fashion* (Indiana University Press, Bloomington, 2010)

André Magnin, Alison de Lima Greene, Alvia J. Wardlaw and Thomas McEvilley, eds, *African Art Now: Masterpieces from the Jean Pigozzi Collection* (Museum of Fine Arts Houston / Merrell, London, 2005)

Els van der Pias and Marious Willemsen, eds, *The Art of African Fashion* (Africa World Press, Inc. / Prince Claus Fund, Trenton, 1998)

Yves Saint Laurent, *Yves Saint Laurent* (The Museum of Modern Art / Clarkson N. Potter, Inc., New York, 1983)

Tank Magazine, vol. 5, issue 5 (2008)

Shade Thomas-Fahm, *Faces of She* (Tegali Communications, 2004)

Carol Tulloch, ed., *Black Style* (V&A Publications, London, 2004)

Carol Woolton, *Fashion For Jewels: 100 Years Of Styles And Icons* (Prestel Publishing, London, 2010)

Main entries are in bold

INDEX

Africa Fashion International
www.afwlive.com

A. Sauvage
asauvage.com

African Mosaique
www.africanmosaique.com

Albertus Swanepoel
albertusswanepoel.com

Alek Wek
www.alekwek.com

Alex Folzi
alexfolzi.ca

Amine Bendriouich
www.ab-cb.com

Angelo Van Mol
www.angelovanmol.com

Anita Quansah
www.anitaquansah.com

Armando Cabral
www.armando-cabral.com

Bestow Elan
www.bestowelan.com

Black Coffee
www.blackcoffee.co.za

Bridget Awosika
www.bridgetawosika.com

Buki Akib
bukiakib.com

Bunmi Koko
www.bunmikoko.com

Casely-Hayford
www.casely-hayford.com

Chris Saunders
www.imagination.co.za
teamuncoolfashion.blogspot.com
chrissaunderssa.blogspot.com

Christie Brown
christiebrownonline.com

David Agbodji
www.heartofbullstudio.com

David Tlale
www.davidtlale.com

Deola Sagoe
www.deolasagoe.net

Duro Olowu
www.duroolowu.com

Emeka Alams
www.before1444.com

Eric Raisina
www.ericraisina.com

FAFA
www.fafakenya.org

Free Peoples Rebellion
www.fprebellion.com

Ger Duany
www.gerduany.com

Gloria Wavamunno
www.facebook.com/pages/GloRia-
WavaMunno/351531069599

Hassan Hajjaj
www.hassan-hajjaj.com

Heni
www.heni.co.za

Iké Udé
www.ikeude.com
thechicindex.com

Ituen Basi
www.ituenbasi.co.uk

Jewel by Lisa
www.jewelbylisa.com.ng

John Kaveke
kaveke.com

Karl-Edwin Guerre
guerreisms.com

Kiko Romeo
www.kikoromeo.com

KLûK CGDT
kluk.co.za

KooRoo
www.kooroos.com

Kwame Brako
www.kwamebrako.com

LaLesso
www.lalesso.com

Loin Cloth & Ashes
www.loinclothandashes.com

Maki Oh
www.maki-oh.com

Mataano
www.mataano.com

Mimi Plange
mimiplange.com

Momo
www.momostyles.com

Nike Davies Okundaye
www.nikeart.com
Nkwo
www.nkwo.co.uk

Oluchi Onweagba
www.oluchi.com

Ozwald Boateng
www.ozwaldboateng.co.uk

Pierre-Antoine Vettorello
www.pierreantoinevettorello.net

Ré Bahia
www.rebahia.com

Samantha Cole London
www.samanthacolelondon.co.uk

Stiaan Louw
stiaanlouw.blogspot.com

Suzaan Heyns
www.suzaanheyns.com

Thula Sindi
www.thulasindi.co.za

Tiffany Amber
www.tiffanyamberng.com

Tsemaye Binitie
www.tsemayebinitie.com

Vlisco
www.vlisco.com

XULY.Bët Funkin' Fashion
www.xulybet.com

CONTACTS

PICTURE CREDITS

Author's Acknowledgements

Thank you to all of the talented designers, models and artists who agreed to be profiled in this book and to the photographers, PRs, agents, stylists and experts who graciously contributed their work, time and effort. Thanks to Iké Udé for writing the Foreword. Thanks to everyone at Prestel, especially Philippa Hurd and Andrew Hansen, for believing in the project, and to Joana Niemeyer and Lisa Sjukur at April for their art direction. Special thanks to Bethann Hardison for her Saturday afternoon conversation; to Nike Davies Okunday for teaching me about adire; and to Sabrina Henry and Chukwunwike Obi for their hard work one especially long, hot day in Lagos. Thanks to Nduka Obaigbena, Penny McDonald and everyone at *ARISE* for their support. Thanks to Bernice at D1, Avinash and Kabir Wadhwani at Temple Muse, Maia Adams, Lola Ogunnaike and Enyinne Owunwanne for their ideas and contacts. Lastly, thank you to the Girl Thursdays and to my family, Peter, Anne and Rebecca, for keeping me sane until the finish line.

UK edition
Front cover: Maki Oh. Photo: Jan Lehner, styling Chukwunwike Obi. Model: Sycha Mubiaya at D1 Models
Back cover: Casely-Hayford. Photo: Scott Trindle. Model: Kinée Diouf at IMG

US edition
Front cover: Duro Oluwu. Photo: John-Paul Pietrus
Back cover: Maki Oh. Photo: Jan Lehner, styling Chukwunwike Obi

Prestel Verlag, Munich
A member of Verlagsgruppe Random House GmbH

Prestel Verlag
Neumarkter Str. 28
81673 Munich
Tel. +49 (0)89 4136-0
Fax +49 (0)89 4136-2335

www.prestel.de

Prestel Publishing Ltd.
4 Bloomsbury Place
London WC1A 2QA
Tel. +44 (0)20 7323-5004
Fax +44 (0)20 7636-8004

Prestel Publishing
900 Broadway, Suite 603
New York, NY 10003
Tel. +1 (212) 995-2720
Fax +1 (212) 995-2733

www.prestel.com

Library of Congress Control Number: 2011929019 (US edition only)

British Library Cataloguing-in-Publication Data: a catalogue record for this book is available from the British Library; Deutsche Nationalbibliothek holds a record of this publication in the Deutsche Nationalbibliografie; detailed bibliographical data can be found under: http://dnb.d-nb.de

Prestel books are available worldwide. Please contact your nearest bookseller or one of the above addresses for information concerning your local distributor.

Editorial direction: Philippa Hurd
Copyedited by: Martha Jay
Production: Friederike Schirge
Art direction: Cilly Klotz
Design and layout: Joana Niemeyer, April
Origination: Reproline Genceller, Munich
Printing and binding: Neografia a. s., Martin
Printed in Slovakia

Verlagsgruppe Random House FSC-DEU-0100
The FSC® -certified paper Hello Fat matt has been supplied by Deutsche Papier, Germany

ISBN 978-3-7913-4696-0 (UK edition)
ISBN 978-3-7913-4579-6 (US edition)